Catlady

Catlady

A Love Letter to Women and Their Cats

Leah Reena Goren

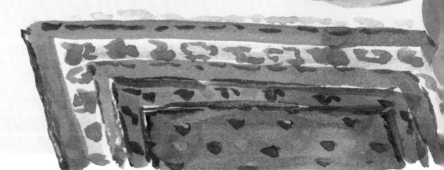

PRESTEL
Munich · London · New York

Contents

Baby Moses

LEAH REENA GOREN

It was decided for me: I was to grow up with poodles. Poodles don't shed, and besides, my dad hated cats. He was allergic, but his distaste for them went beyond the potential for itchy eyes or a runny nose. The sight alone of any neighborhood stray made his face twist in disgust. If it wandered too close, he shooed it away with a loud *pssss*.

Our first dog was Molly, born to be a show dog but rejected for the tiny tuft of black fur on her otherwise white coat. As kids we would search for the black curl under her ear to show off her ruined career. "*See?*"

After Molly there was Jamie, and then Ellie, and then Tova. Tova is still alive, completely blind in the one eye she has left, sniffing her way around the house we grew up in.

My dad always talked about Homer, his childhood schnauzer, who was trained to sit still at the command, "Treif," the Milk-Bone balanced on his nose gobbled up as soon as someone said, "Kosher." But there had once been a cat in the family who was rarely mentioned. "April, she was snow white—a very sexy, beautiful cat," my grandmother Cherie recalled as she sipped her evening glass of vodka on the rocks. "We had a picture window and the toms would line up outside. She was the neighborhood hussy. She had more kittens than any cat I ever knew. No one thought to get cats fixed in those days. April," she continued, "would stay up in Ellen's room all day long while Ellen went to school. She wouldn't talk to anybody else. When Ellen came home, she would hop off of Ellen's bed and come to the top of the staircase, majestically look down on you, turn up her nose, and go back to bed. She was really a brat."

Ellen was my dad's sister, older and overachieving. "They had the same IQ," my grandmother loves to say, "but he wanted to be the class clown." Ellen grew up to be a corporate lawyer while my dad barely attended college. And though he was allergic, there was no way April would ever be rehomed. It makes sense why he continued to *pssss* at cats into adulthood. Childhood cat trauma.

Unbelievably, I didn't have a face-to-face encounter with a cat until the summer I was twenty-two. It's kind of like how I hadn't tried a cheeseburger till around then, either. Some things just happened later. I moved into a small, dark two-bedroom apartment in Williamsburg, Brooklyn, with my best friend, Taylor. (It feels childish now to qualify our friendship as *best,* but I still can't not say it.) Our apartment faced a damp alley where mosquitoes were rampant, and without air-conditioning or window screens we were bitten all summer. I don't know why we didn't remedy the situation; we were young and unconcerned.

One day Taylor brought home a gray kitten she had found on the street. Knowing I was allergic and tired of her thoughtless, near-constant antics, she promised it would be gone by the next day, and then promptly left for work. Home alone with the kitten, I didn't know what I was supposed to do with it. I was afraid of sneezing. I wasn't sure how to pick it up. But it was so cute. I cautiously let it roam around my bedroom until it fell asleep at my feet, and together we curled up on my mattress set right on the slanted wood floor. My first day with a cat! Thrilling. I took a ton of photos, tiny and pixelated on my BlackBerry, which I then drew from in wavy black ink.

I loved these drawings and I didn't want to stop. The cat was the perfect symbol. Dogs—I knew dogs. Everyone knew dogs. It may have been my own unfamiliarity, but cats seemed like they could be or represent *anything*, something more in line with human emotions, perhaps. I typed "cat" into Google Images and drew a dozen more, assembling my favorites into a careful square. I added color and had it printed onto my first silk scarf.

I started noticing cats everywhere in art. I found Vera Neumann's cheery mid-century-style cats on linen tea towels and napkins, and Niki de Saint Phalle's mosaic cat sculpture back home in San Diego. I realized I had spent my whole childhood looking at a watercolor of a black cat by my mom, titled *Bootsie at the Egyptian Apartments*. I followed Balthus's fascination, from his childhood cat to his arresting paintings of young girls and theirs. I saw myself in Will Barnet's contemplative portraits: a woman reading calmly in bed, her white cat resting on her lap; a woman dressed serenely in lavender, a calico slung over her shoulder.

And there they were in old photos, too, the companions of artists in a time that looked more perfect. I fell in love with Celia Birtwell's bold florals and also her life—the way she collaborated beautifully with her fashion designer husband and played muse to David Hockney, all the while accompanied in the studio by her cat Blanche. I saw an aged, wise Sonia Delaunay grinning alongside a long-haired cat. In one snapshot, Matisse's assistant Annelies Nelck took a break from installing his paper cut-outs to pet a reclining tabby.

These women were all me. I didn't have a cat, but this was how *I* felt. The cat was an accessory to a quiet moment. An image of a solitary woman could mean any number of things, but a woman shown with a cat is safe to indulge in her inner monologue. A woman with a cat is safe to be alone. She is home.

I drew more and more cats and found ways to transfer them onto fabric. In my screen printing class I burned a grouping of grace-ful line drawings onto a screen, and squeegeed them out onto canvas bags. At home, with less equipment at my disposal, I made a stamp out of a rubber block, carving in a graphic cat head silhouette. I painted my screen printing ink onto the raised shape, which gave each print a brushy, textured look, and began stamping it onto fabric. I spaced each cat head evenly, like a classic polka dot pattern. I took the fabric and sewed myself a loose, baby doll dress—sleeveless with a short, gathered skirt. I shared it online, and it turned out the Internet loved cats, too; I ended up spending so many hours over the next several years selling and handmaking these dresses. I wasn't a fashion designer and I was barely a seamstress, but I was a college student who couldn't say no to an opportunity for self-employment. By the time I graduated, I had licensed the black cat block print to Anthropologie and they had produced 5,500 dresses. Somehow I had become an illustrator who specialized in cat prints, and I wasn't even sure how much I knew about them.

=^-^=

I saw his photo online first—a low-res rectangle of what looked like a naked mole rat with bat ears, crouched on tiny legs barely large enough to support his weeks-old body, his skin pink and nearly hairless. He was a breed called Devon rex that I sought out for its hypoallergenic reputation; their short, wavy hair allegedly shed very little, allowing lower dander levels.

I named him Moses. *Baby Moses, Prince of Egypt* I thought to myself, finding strange comfort in a biblical reference that brought me back to my loathed days in Hebrew school. Baby Moses, sailing down the Nile bundled in his little basket. I nestled my own Moses into an old sweatshirt, fashioning it into a sling so I could carry him around the apartment while I worked. He would climb into my arms to sleep, insisting nowhere else was as comfortable. At night he nestled between my legs or under the crook of an arm or right on top of my pillow, curled around my head like a fancy turban. I am not a cuddler—I like to be left alone while I sleep—but I learned how to be still with him.

Moses loved my then-boyfriend Dylan, as well as friends who came over a lot. He had a friend of his own, too. Sometimes, if I heard a scratch on the door, I'd let him out to play with Thunder Paws. Thunder Paws was a large tabby with green eyes, a former outdoor cat who, now confined indoors, spent a lot of time roaming the halls between the second and fourth floors. He belonged to an upstairs neighbor, a friendly Australian woman with tanned skin and a short black bob, whom I perceived as at least five years older than me, especially after she mentioned her husband. In a building teeming with young gentrifiers, any difference in age felt as palpable as it did throughout high school and college. I personally could not imagine ever uttering the word *husband*.

An anxious first-time cat owner, I would hover in the doorway while Moses was roaming the halls. Some evenings my neighbor would come downstairs and chat while our cats chased each other up and down the stairs. Leaning against the wall in the foyer, she'd flip through photos on her phone and show me what she'd spent the day working on as a photo retoucher for the Metropolitan Museum of Art's archive.

Toward the end of winter, Moses and I were huddled on the floor next to the heater. The apartment was terribly cold unless we stayed right there. We spent a lot of time there, me with my back against the bed frame, him on his little patchwork cushion I had sewed for him. Moses sneezed. I wasn't sure I had seen him sneeze before, at least not like this. He lurched, and then his body froze, his mouth open and lips turned up in a snarl. Drool dripped onto the floor. "You OK?!" I exclaimed, laughing it off. And then it happened again.

I threw my loose, gray striped coat on over my T-shirt and leggings and we were in the backseat of a car service, heading to our vet in nearby Queens. I took a long walk through an unfamiliar neighborhood awaiting a diagnosis, learning finally that the sneezes were in fact seizures. Moses was moved to a better-equipped vet nearby, and then to a fancy twenty-four-hour vet in midtown Manhattan. Days passed, X-rays were conducted and tests were run. I jotted down notes onto scraps of paper when the veterinarians called me during the day. I took the train uptown to visit Moses at night. I went

out for drinks with friends to hold onto a sense of normalcy, pushing down the familiar feeling that I alone was falling apart. I gave the go-ahead for an expensive MRI; I spent my mid-twenties savings on him.

The MRI revealed there was something wrong with his brain, but they didn't know what. I could pay to have a sample tested by experts in California, but that would take more days, and more money to keep him alive in kitty urgent care. He was suffering.

Our situation was not unique. In a dim, windowless basement room, we heard the muffled sounds of other families saying their goodbyes through the thin walls. I held him like a baby in my arms, like I always had. He was my baby, my first cat. Baby Moses. I was all he had in this world. His eyes pleaded with me, in pain.

This was it. I wanted so badly to remember him, knowing the moment would inevitably fade into a melancholy snapshot. His body was warm, heavy, and limp. I felt his ripply fur around my fingers, soft as a newborn lamb, and I thought *I will forget this.*

It is very unsettling seeing someone in a way they've never been. Moses, defeated. A week ago he had been racing from one end to the other in my railroad apartment. I have a memory of my dad in the ICU after his car accident, pink and bloated head to toe. Until that moment, he had been a small athletic man, lithe and tanned. My fourteen-year-old self took one look at the pink man in a coma and, bursting into tears, fled into the hallway. I had been taken off guard by my reaction, as if it had happened without my consent.

My dad's death was anything but straightforward. When he woke up from his coma, he was a completely different person. Over the next year, I slowly and silently mourned the loss of his past self. The tracheostomy gave him a new voice, brain damage gave him a new personality, and lingering injuries prevented him from walking. As far as I was concerned, he wasn't my dad. The brain damage rendered him aggressive and violent, even from the confines of a wheelchair, and my mom made the difficult decision to send him to live with his parents in Philadelphia in order to protect my sister and me. Eventually, when my mom hung up the phone one evening and called my sister and me into the living room to tell us daddy had died, it had felt like little more than a final plot point—the ending of a movie I hadn't felt like finishing. I went back to the den and resumed chatting with a couple of cute boys from school on AOL Instant Messenger.

I lived for the next decade without giving death a second thought. The childhood poodles had passed, of course, but of very old age while I was off at college. I was young, and my own end felt distant, if not impossible. Sitting with Moses in the basement, for the first time I visualized the exact moment between being alive and being dead. It was so tragically, bewilderingly clear-cut.

Dylan wanted to stay and hold Moses while they gave him the injection. I left the room, though I might as well have been there for the amount of times I've sobbingly conjured an image of what his last moments must have been like. Upstairs, under fluorescent lighting, I paid the $6,000 balance with my credit card and took the train home.

The days that followed had made little sense. I hadn't had a year of separation or the cushion of my teenage mind to help me this time. Setting a glass of water down on my dresser reminded me that Moses wouldn't jump up onto the dresser, drink from the glass, and then knock it over. I placed a couple of plants on the windowsill because there was no one to sit there and watch the birds. I opened one of the storage drawers in my bed frame so that no one came running, eager to bury himself into the soft piles of sweaters.

One day I heard a faint noise in the hallway and opened the door to find Thunder Paws. I let him in, and then went into a kitchen drawer to scoop out a generous handful of treats. "I don't need these anymore," I said, dropping them onto the hardwood floor in front of him. I went back to my room and lay down in the last sunbeam of late afternoon while he searched the apartment. When he was done, he came and sat facing me at the edge of the bed. "Moses doesn't live here anymore," I told him, and then we lay there in silence.

I don't think about Moses very much anymore, just as I knew I wouldn't. Enough time has passed that I have to find a drawing to jog my memory. It's dated 2014. I have two cats now, who have taught me no life lessons thus far. I find joy in watching them wrestle, pounce on rubber bands, and sit atop bits of cardboard—acts I am fully aware would be less than delightful to anyone who has not lived with them. I know they too will leave me one day and my heart will be broken all over again. Luckily it still feels distant, if not impossible.

—

On Kitten Rescue

AN INTERVIEW WITH
HANNAH SHAW AND SONJA LUESCHEN

Some months after my cat Moses died, before I adopted Aaron and Lacy, but after a summer stint cat-sitting a fickle calico named Passiflora, I decided to foster a litter of six-week-old kittens. They were jet black and wildly fuzzy, wriggling around my Brooklyn bedroom like caterpillars on the loose. There were four of them, but I had only two hands, and the more I lost control the more they seemed to multiply. Just as I stopped one from peeing in my large potted rubber tree, two others would climb in and begin digging holes.

In retrospect, I had no idea what I was doing, and I could have used the guidance of someone like Hannah Shaw. You may know Shaw as Kitten Lady, a humane educator who travels the U.S. teaching about neonatal care for kittens and has developed an arsenal of educational media and training resources, all in the service of saving tiny orphan kittens. Shaw is also the founder of Orphan Kitten Club (OKC), a nonprofit rescue and adoption organization, and volunteers much of her time when she's not on the road fostering the kittens in the nursery.

If this sounds like a lot for one woman to take on, well, it is. In perpetually warm San Diego kitten season never stops, but Shaw is assisted by her partner and fiancé, cat photographer Andrew Marttila, as well as Sonja Lueschen, the program manager of Orphan Kitten Club. I was lucky enough to run into them in Anza-Borrego, California, while they were taking a much-needed moment off from saving tiny lives to enjoy the sun and a big bloom of wildflowers.

Shaw: I have been involved in animal welfare since I was twelve years old. I advocated for farm animals, circus animals, and animals in laboratories, but I wasn't involved with cat welfare until ten years ago—my cat Coco is turning ten next week. She was the first kitten I ever found. I was twenty-one years old, had just graduated college, and moved to Philadelphia. In a park in North Philly, I spotted a kitten in a tree. It blew my mind. I had no idea there were kittens in trees. I couldn't figure out why she was there and I couldn't figure out what kind of help she needed, but I knew that I cared about animals and that was enough to propel me into action. So I climbed the tree. Her little body was so small and limp, and she was so weak. I reached out on a branch, got her, put her in my shirt, and shimmied back down the tree. I felt triumphant for about three seconds and then absolutely panicked. I didn't know what to do or what she needed. But I took her home and now she celebrates her ten-year birthday next week. She was my starter kitten, and I always say it's amazing that out of every cat who could have been my first cat I got the very best one. She's the greatest cat in the world. Coco is my ride or die.

After that day in the park I became more aware of the landscape around me and I started noticing cats all over the place in Philly. I saw kittens everywhere and began rescuing orphaned kittens. People started finding out I was doing this and they would call me when they found kittens. And so I always worked with kittens—I was never involved with adult cats. It built and built until I ended up moving to North Carolina. That is where everything shifted for me. My heart was broken as I became involved in rural North Carolina's shelters, and everything I do now is about trying to piece it all back together. At the time there were eleven shelters in North Carolina that still used gas chambers. Until then, I had only worked with kittens from the street, and it was really disturbing seeing what was happening in the shelters. I would go there and let them know that I had the skill set and ability to help with orphan kittens. If they did get orphan kittens, of course they would never save them. They were not even really able to help healthy adult cats, much less kittens. Through a lot of trial and error and a lot of passion and what little

research I had been able to do, I gained a lot of experience working with orphan kittens.

My career began shifting toward cat welfare. I started working for cat welfare organizations—policy work, national fund-raising, liaising with shelters all over the country on their behalf. I learned that the small rural shelters in North Carolina were just one way of being a shelter; there are also really huge therapy shelters with a different set of issues related to their urban settings.

All this time, rescuing kittens was something that I'd done myself. People would say, "Oh my friend Hannah—she's such a cat lady!" I would correct them and say, "No, not really, I'm a kitten lady! I just do kittens!" If someone found an adult cat I would tell them there are plenty of people who can help. People who are willing to work with neonatal orphan kittens are a really rare breed. I tried to let people know if I was working with shelters or friends or other people in the movement they could count on me for this because it was a niche thing.

Kitten Lady and my ability to do it as a job happened so serendipitously. I was working for a national cat advocacy organization and feeling pangs of wanting to do more kitten advocacy, but there were no opportunities like that. Kittens were really not a priority—and still are not a priority—in a national sense in sheltering. At the time, Instagram was in its really early stages, and I decided to make a page because I thought my friends were probably really sick of seeing me post photos of kittens all the time. I just called it Kitten Lady. To my surprise it started growing. At work, I was beginning to train people in what I was doing with kittens and creating educational materials just for when I was traveling. I put some of that out on social media simply to save time. I'd have friends who would come to me and say, "Hey, I got a kitten—what do I do?!" I would create a video just for them. I made a video for a friend explaining how to make slurries—a mix of formula and wet food—to feed a kitten. I put it on YouTube and all of a sudden it started getting picked up. I realized no one was creating these resources and I could be the one to create them. I wish I had a buddy who had taught me this stuff. I wish there had been somebody who had explained what to do with a kitten who doesn't want to eat when it's midnight and no one's around to help! I decided I was going to use this weird social platform to be that buddy to others.

It has grown in a way I could never have possibly anticipated but it makes me so happy because I always really felt that kittens would be the final frontier of feline welfare in shelters. We've done so much to educate the public about spay and neuter, owner retention, behavior programs, and even feral cat programs, but kittens are by far the most vulnerable feline population in a shelter. They enter shelters at the largest rates, and they are the most euthanized in shelters. People just don't know that. We don't talk about it. People don't realize when we talk about no-kill shelters, no-kill by definition doesn't include kittens under eight weeks old. No-kill is defined as a live release rate for 90 percent of healthy animals, and healthy is defined as animals over eight weeks of age. You can say you're a no-kill shelter and still have thousands of kittens being euthanized. Everything I do is about working with shelters and teaching them, training them, and trying to recruit foster parents for them.

Kitten Lady has grown into a collection of educational resources for people who want to learn how to take care of kittens or about feline welfare issues that particularly pertain to kittens and community cats (which of course have so much to do with kittens). I try to use my platform to inform people about what's going on in a way that's palatable enough that they'll watch. That's why it's all very cute, fluffy, and adorable—but that's almost a trap! I want to get people interested in the message and inspire them to actually do something about it. I do trainings, I teach more than fifty classes a year all over the country and internationally. I have two books and over a hundred videos on my YouTube channel.

One of the things I'm proudest of is a series of educational

Kitten Nursery Care Routine for Neonates!
58,350 views

booklets that are now used in over five hundred shelters. In 2016 I conducted a survey of foster parents to find out how their experience was, and one of the most jaw-dropping things I learned was that more than half of the foster parents said they were given no written training materials from their shelter. I wanted to fill those gaps. People should have resources when they're rescuing so that they have relevant information and don't feel alone. Nobody is born knowing this stuff. It does not come naturally. The guilt and sorrow people feel when something goes wrong and they feel like they could have done something differently is so visceral that I want people to feel like they are coming to rescue with a full tool kit and support. The booklets lead to the apex of everything I ever wanted to do, my book *Tiny but Mighty*. It has everything in it. Well, not everything—I'm still learning. There's support for every single thing you might experience. The booklets are 12 pages and the book is 336 pages! It's very thorough.

Orphan Kitten Club is the rescue part of what I do. After fostering for other organizations, it became very clear to me that I was going to have to start my own nonprofit. The types of cases I wanted to take on just aren't common enough for anybody else to be willing to try. We take the kittens that even the best shelters won't take—kittens with congenital deformities, premature kittens, special needs babies, and critically sick kittens. Running my own rescue organization means we can decide on the population we want to focus on and the level of care that we want to provide. People ask how many kittens we have, or how many kittens we saved last year—most organizations measure their impact in numbers of lives, which is useful but not how we measure the value of our work. We take on highly specific, dedicated, challenging cases and measure our impact more in the stories of the individuals affected rather than through raw data. If I wanted to be able to say I had fifty kittens in my house I could, but they'd all have to be healthy, robust kittens. I'd much rather have six really complicated kittens that I can fully focus on, and be the only person who is willing to do it. We're even pushing the veterinarians we work with to learn new skills because a lot of them have never worked with the types of cases that we have. They are surprised to see somebody willing to invest the time and money to work with these babies. We're a pretty weird organization, but one that is founded on the idea of maintaining a stubborn hope for positive outcomes even in the most complicated neonatal kittens.

Sonja has been such a help because she's as passionate about kittens and kitten care as I am. Without her invaluable work managing the day-to-day needs of our nonprofit, I wouldn't be able to focus on my role as educator. She does so much.

Before kittens, I used to work with kids. Kids are so cool because they're innately compassionate. They inherently understand why this stuff is important. It's been surprising to see that many of the viewers on my YouTube channel are children. A lot of kids come to my events with tons of questions. It was only natural that I ended up writing a children's book, *Kitten Lady's Big Book of Little Kittens*, at the same time I was working on *Tiny but Mighty*. *Kitten Lady's Big Book of Little Kittens* is a story about a foster kitten's journey from rescue to adoption. Hopefully readers will be inspired to go on a similar journey once they are older. At the end of the book there's a note to parents, guardians, teachers, and librarians about how to actually get involved in this work. Fostering is something that's so wonderful for families to do during the summer because kitten season happens when school is out. The old-school mentality of wanting your kids to experience the miracle of life by letting your dog have puppies is really not the best place for us right now. Instead, why not let parents or guardians show their kids the differences they can make by fostering even one litter of kittens or one mom with babies during the summer? It makes a big impact on the lives of the animals as well as the kids.

A couple of years ago, a little girl came to one of my events and said, "I want to start fostering Beanie Babies so that I can prove

to my mom that I have what it takes to foster kittens." I said, "Do it!" She started making videos where she weighed the Beanie Babies every day and nursed them with a fake bottle. Now she's fourteen and she's fostered forty-seven kittens in the last two years. It's amazing to see young people get involved; experience is everything. Every kitten I take on gives me something I use to save another kitten in the future. If you start fostering as a kid, you're going to be so, so skilled at helping save lives by the time you're my age. I didn't start until I was twenty-one. And by the time you're my age this will be commonplace in animal welfare. We are working so hard on solving so many other issues that now people can turn their focus toward kittens. There are nurseries starting to pop up in a lot of the bigger shelters in major cities. But it's still very, very early stages. Even in terms of research for kittens there's not a strong focus on feline pediatrics. I never imagined I'd be speaking at a vet conference—I'm not a vet—but I did because there's just not a lot of knowledge about care and husbandry for kittens out there. But I see change. The shelters I used to go to in North Carolina no longer have gas chambers as they've been outlawed there. The one shelter in particular that really broke my heart was bulldozed and replaced by a much nicer one. Things are changing, and people are learning, but you can't change what you don't know about, and you can't know what you don't talk about, so my life is spent trying to get people to talk about it.

It's been a dream to get kittens on the scene. When I started doing this it felt like nobody even imagined that it was possible or worthwhile to consider helping these little ones. I really like proving people wrong. I like taking on cases that people think are not going to be viable and then succeeding, because I think only through that curiosity and stubbornness and hopeful perspective can you find out what you can actually achieve. Being able to show people what is possible has been a really positive part of the project, and in turn they are willing to try more things, too. If jobs didn't exist, this is still what I would be doing. This is what I love. This is what I care about. This is what I'm here to do.

One of the best things that rescuers can do to set themselves up for success long term is to let themselves find joy in the process. So much of it is joyful, but we often don't let ourselves really feel that, and feel that we're making an impact. Bringing joy and levity into rescue is something I'd like to see more of. Setting yourself up for success means having measurable goals you can achieve. *I'm going to save this animal, and then I'm going to celebrate.* Or, *I'm just going to get this kitten's eyes looking better,* and then when you do you lie on the floor with them and you look at them and think *wow, life is amazing, I'm proud of myself, and I'm happy for this individual.* Those things are very healing.

Lueschen: After years of being an antiques dealer, I found myself yearning to make an impact within my community. I had always wanted to work with animals, but I had no professional experience. At twenty-six I went back to school to get my veterinary assistant certificate. At the end of the nine-month program, we were all placed in internships. I vividly remember my teacher telling me that I was more of a private practice girl and wouldn't do well at the animal shelter. I wanted to prove her wrong and challenge myself, so I pushed to intern at our local Humane Society. The first two weeks of my internship were at the kitten nursery. It was a life-changing experience. It was there that I found my passion for neonatal care. I can still remember literally shaking when I bottle-fed my first baby kitten. I was so nervous! I quickly got the hang of things and was hired during my internship. That is when I started my career working as a nursery caregiver, bottle-feeding kittens forty hours a week. It was a dream job and I am forever grateful for the skills I learned there.

I basically have the greatest job on the planet at Orphan Kitten Club. I get to work hands-on with the kittens in our nursery and also handle the backend of our nonprofit. My responsibilities in the nursery include transferring kittens into our rescue, coordinating medical care, and finding the perfect adopters. The other side of my job includes donor acknowledgment, volunteer management, communications with the public, TNR (Trap Neuter Return), and other lifesaving programs.

The day never stops in our nursery! Our kittens get around-the-clock care from Hannah, her partner, Andrew, and myself. Our nursery is small but impactful. We have a neonatal room with two kitten incubators for the babies zero to three weeks old and a social-ization room with a custom-made kitten activity center for the big kids. We generally have two or three litters at a time. We focus on very tiny orphan neonates, some only a few hours old, as well as special needs kittens. Our kittens need to be stimulated and fed twenty-four hours a day. The tiniest kittens require feedings every two hours, even during the night. The care routine for the kittens is always the same. Stimulate them to go potty (this is something their mother would be doing for them), weigh them, feed them, and put them back in the incubator. Some of our more critical cases may require supportive care such as subcutaneous fluids and even tube feeding. It can sometimes be stressful working with such tiny kittens but we have an incredible team and access to exceptional medical care.

Working in animal welfare comes at a price. I learned about compassion fatigue very early on in my career. I can remember having pretty much all of the signs of classic burnout. My emotions were all over the place. One minute I would be feeling an immense sense of grief and then that feeling would turn into anger. I just felt like nobody cared or understood what these poor animals were going through. I would obsess about the kittens on my days off and text coworkers asking for updates. It was an all-encompassing sadness. My boyfriend and family noticed this change in me and helped me work through my intense sorrow. I focused my spare time on my hobbies. I made art, cooked elaborate vegan meals, and got lost in books. I made space for myself again. I realized that I can't change

the world with anger and learned the importance of self-care.

Aside from this, I have so many lovely kitten memories! One of my favorite memories with OKC was when I had a slumber party with a litter lovingly referred to as The Pizza Boyz. It was right before Jumbo Slice and Deep Dish were going to their forever home. I wanted to spend as much time with them as possible, so I decided to spend the night in the kitten room. I made a blanket fort, which lasted about two minutes before the kittens demolished it. I remember I put on the documentary *Kedi* about the cats of Istanbul. Jumbo and DD were totally mesmerized by the cats on the screen. When I woke up in the morning both of them were curled up in my sleeping bag. It was the best slumber party I've ever been to.

Outside of OKC, I'm basically a vintage cat collectible hoarder. Vintage cat photos are my personal favorite. I have been collecting vernacular photography since I was in high school. I have always had framed photographs of strangers lining the walls of my home. I'm just so drawn to unique faces and I really appreciate a beautifully composed shot. A few years ago, I went to an estate sale and found an entire photo album full of photos of the family's tabby cat. It was so hilarious and heartwarming at the same time. That's when I really started to focus on feline photos. I comb through estate sales, swap meets, thrift stores, and the Internet in search of vintage photos of other people's cats. I just love that back when a snapshot was actually a precious thing, and not just digital data, people still chose to photograph their kitty companions. I love sharing my feline finds and I hope to one day have a book published of my collection.

If you love cats and consider yourself a cat lady or cat man, please help the cats in your community. Don't just talk the talk—walk the walk and make an impact locally. Volunteer at your local shelter, become a foster parent, donate to a cat rescue, or learn about TNR and help sterilize a colony in your neighborhood. There are countless ways to make a difference and it is our responsibility as cat people to help.

Hannah Shaw is a humane educator and founder of the nonprofit rescue organization Orphan Kitten Club. Her books include *Tiny but Mighty* and *Kitten Lady's Big Book of Little Kittens*.

Sonja Lueschen is a kitten rescuer, the program manager for Orphan Kitten Club, and a collector of vintage feline treasures.

Hello Kitty

It is impossible to discuss cats without recalling childhood trips to the Sanrio store, a brightly lit, pastel-hued haven among the otherwise dark ground-floor shops at our local mall. Inside I lusted after rubbery wallets and cubes of fruity gum, all emblazoned with the Hello Kitty character. Sanrio is a Japanese gift company dating back to 1960, whose products have always been embellished with cute cartoons. In 1974, designer Yuko Shimizu added Hello Kitty to the line. Since then, she's become a global sensation, decorating countless products and even cafés and theme parks. But the biggest surprise of all: Sanrio insists that Hello Kitty is not a cat. She's a cartoon, a friend, and a little girl.

I Love Cat

JUSTINA BLAKENEY

He was so sweet, and despite being long and lean, he was also cuddly. He nestled up to me in the mornings in a way that was so warm and loving. He was pensive and kind of a loner, but that fit my bubbly, gregarious personality in a yin-yang kind of way. There was only one problem, he had a cat. Oy.

I have a hairy history with cats. I am very allergic to them. One of my earliest and most vivid memories is stretching up to reach the doorknob of my parents' bedroom during my first cat-induced asthma attack. But I also have a hairy history with men. So when I found one whom I really liked, I knew I'd need to work out the whole cat thing, because this dude was really into his cat, and I was really into this dude.

His name is Luda. The cat, not the man. The man is Jason. Luda was three years old when Jason and I started dating. I lived in Brooklyn, New York, at the time, and Jason lived in Los Angeles at the Brewery Art Colony. When I went to LA, I went with Claritin and Ventolin in tow like two BFFs. Jason's place was an open loft; there were always artworks in progress: robots made from found objects, half-painted canvases, defunct computers, and Jackson Pollock-style cat hair smatterings EVERYwhere—an artsy, bachelor pad kind of vibe. Luda was an indoor-outdoor kitty. He ruled the Brewery, and then would pop back into the loft and rule thepad, too. As long as I took my meds and didn't touch the cat, it was tolerable—a sneezy, itchy, tight throat, teary-eyed kinda tolerable, but hey, I was in love—and I had tolerated worse from hairy creatures in the past.

Two years into our long-distance relationship I moved to Los Angeles. I lived on my own for the first time in a tiny Spanish-style bungalow. It had a living room, a narrow galley kitchen, a boxy little bedroom, and a bathroom squished into 450 square feet. I decorated it to the max—covered it in boho, botanical textiles, funky wall coverings, tchotchkes galore, and about forty-five houseplants. When Luda, Jason, and I decided to take things to the next level and move in together, I had illusions of relegating Lil' Lu to the living room and kitchen. I would have rules. He could not come onto the bed. He could not be on the kitchen table. Seemed reasonable enough to me.

As Jason and Luda began to unpack their things, within about two hours it was made abundantly clear that Luda was not much of a rule follower. He wasn't even like a pet, *really*. He was more like a boyfriend's brother who was jobless, girlfriendless, kinda grumpy with zero sense of boundaries or manners, and staying on your living room sofa for an undetermined period of time. We kept Luda inside the bungalow for the first six weeks so he could adjust to his new surroundings. He did not like this. He tried to escape EVERY SINGLE TIME the front door opened even a little bit, which paralyzed me with fear because our new place was on a pretty busy little street.

He curled up on my pillow at night and "combed" my bushy hair with his paws at first light. He swatted at my legs for food when he was peckish. He walked all over my keyboard, even sat on my laptop while I was working. He snoozed in the middle of the kitchen table. He had fleas and worms. He humped my leg (cats do that?!?!). He left little nests of filth in his favorite sleeping nooks—anything new was particularly cozy to him, especially fabric finds from the flea market (rugs, clothing, pillows, scarves, etc.). He drank from the toilet bowl. The smell of his food made me gag—and don't get me started on the litter box. *I* began to try to escape every time the front door opened.

But alas, the six weeks quickly passed. We got rid of the fleas and worms, and once he was able to roam outdoors the litter box disappeared as well. Much to my surprise, I no longer had to take daily allergy meds. I had somehow adjusted to him, and he, perhaps,

to me. As a show of good faith, he wasn't big on eating houseplants, or shredding textiles, which made me really happy because I was really big on houseplants and textiles. And though he still combed my hair at first light, which Jason insisted was a sign of affection, we began to coexist and to share Jason's love. He had enough to go around.

Eventually, we moved to a bigger bungalow. Jason and I got hitched and had a baby girl. Ida was an early talker, and her first word, even before she could crawl or walk was "Kitteh," and she squealed it with glee as she pointed at Luda as he scurried under her high-chair. From the moment she was strong enough to hold her own head up (and when he'd let her) she nestled her face in Luda's soft, furry belly. He was kind to her, even when she annoyed the hell out of him. Six years later, Ida wears cat ears and cat tails to school, sings in meows, and calls Luda her little brother.

Luda and I have lived together for ten years now. He still enjoys sharing bed pillows and testing out any new fabrics I bring home, but he has his corners, and I have mine. Our relationship has shifted over the years. He is less of an annoying couch crasher and more like an old childhood friend: we've been through a lot together, we somehow understand each other, and, unlike Jason, he will get cozy with me to binge-watch *This Is Us*. I'm not sure we'd automatically be friends had we met today, but we have history, and he's part of the family.

As I type this, Luda is sitting not so patiently to my right, meowing for foowmke ;;;;;;;jnn'12hwiurhpncnq[wn ;rjhw qr[qrq

Well, he has never stopped walking over my keyboard as I work, but I've grown to love his little silly mannerisms and even, once in a while, enjoy his company. I may not be a cat lady, but I am this cat's lady. And I love the little fucker.

≳•≲

Justina Blakeney is a Los Angeles–based designer and the author of the *New York Times* best-selling book, *The New Bohemians*.

Brigitte Bardot

"I am really a cat transformed into a woman. I purr, I scratch. And sometimes I bite," meowed Brigitte Bardot, the French actress and 1960s style icon. She loved animals and was photographed with countless cats. In 1973 Bardot quit acting to work full-time as an animal rights activist, ultimately founding the Brigitte Bardot Foundation in 1986. In 1992 the foundation opened a shelter in a large abandoned mansion in the woods of Normandy, France. Called La Mare Auzou, it is host to an entire farm of animals, including horses, sheep, goats, cows, pigs, chickens, hundreds of dogs, and nearly seven hundred cats. The cats fill ten different areas, and even have their own outdoor aviaries so that they can enjoy the garden.

On Breeding

AN INTERVIEW WITH NAOMI KOLB

When I tell people that my cat Lacy is a retired breeding cat, they usually say, "Oh, poor dear, she's probably had such a rough life," to which I respond, "No, I don't think so, she lived with a nice family in Montana and was very well taken care of."

Naomi Kolb is the owner of Montana Devons, a small family cattery breeding Devon rex cats in Missoula, Montana. The breed originated in Buckfastleigh, Devonshire, England, in 1960, and is most genetically similar to Cornish rex and sphynx cats. Devon rexes are special for many reasons, but most notable is their appearance. Their fur coats are very short, soft, and wavy because they are missing the outer layer of long guard hairs that most cats have. Because of this they shed very little and are often sought by people with allergies like me.

Moses came from Naomi. I e-mailed her when he died, and she mentioned that his mother, Lacy, would be retiring in a couple years and would need a new home and asked if I was interested in adopting her. Without question, I said yes, mentally penning it into my two-year plan. When the time came I took one of the kittens from her last litter as well, thinking Lacy would want some company in retirement. I imagined it had been tough for Lacy to say goodbye to all her kids over the years (I knew it probably wasn't) and hoped she'd finally experience motherhood as it should be, raising her son from infancy to adulthood (I'm not sure she has any notion that they are related, though they certainly love each other). I would have let her name him, too, but I don't know if she grasps that concept, either. I named him Aaron, an admittedly silly name for a cat, after the biblical brother of Moses.

I've felt some of the greatest joy and heartbreak in my life because of Naomi, yet I have never met her—all of my cats have caught a ride on Delta straight to JFK—or even corresponded with her in much detail. Our past e-mails mostly have subjects like "Vet info" or attachments of sixteen kitten photos. I had so many questions for her. How did she learn to breed? What was delivering the first litter like? Had it been hard to say goodbye to Lacy, or the countless other cats over the years?

Kolb: I've had cats my entire life except a short amount of time after I moved across country. That was rectified after about six months when I was able to get one of my childhood cats from my mom's to take back with me.

Growing up we had litters of kittens every few years because my parents were always slow to get any new cats spayed— don't be like my parents in this respect, get your pets spayed and neutered!—and I raised mice, rats, guinea pigs, rabbits, and a plethora of other animals. So breeding animals really wasn't anything new to me when we decided to establish our cattery. It was more like a natural progression once we got a house and adequate space and everything.

I'm drawn to the Devon rex for the personality, the looks, and—who am I kidding—the minimal shedding doesn't hurt, either. But by far, their personalities are what first hooked me. The description that almost never fails is a cross between a monkey and a dog, in a catsuit. It is hard to walk around our house without having at least one cat hurl themselves at you in attempts to sit on your shoulder like a parrot. They are comical in playing and chasing each other around. They love high spaces, and getting into trouble, especially eating things they shouldn't. And they have an innate need for attention and companionship. Life is never lonely or boring with Devon rexes.

I will never forget our very first Devon litter because it was definitely an experience. It was the middle of the night and we had the queen in the kitten room (our master bathroom), she woke us up meowing and scratching at the door, so we let her out. She promptly

jumped into bed with my husband and me, crawled under the covers between us, halfway down the bed, and proceeded to purr. My husband was petting her when suddenly the sheet was wet; she was in labor and the first sac had burst. I grabbed a bunch of towels and we got them under her. So there she is, neither of us have any desire to attempt to move her back to her box or lie on the tile bathroom floor with her, so she gets her way and gives birth to her kittens in our bed. Luckily there were only three of them, and it took about an hour and a half to have them all. Then we were finally able to get back to sleep that night before work the next morning.

Breeding takes a village—seriously just like with children—and having a good support team of mentors, vets, and fellow breeders is imperative to being successful. A lot of what I learned first was through my mentor and other breeders, and then just from experience. Now with everything being on the Internet it makes it much easier to learn about all of the above and connect with other breeders around the world. Having worldwide contacts at the tip of your fingers is helpful because just when you think you've seen it all in the breeding world, something new will pop up and throw you for a loop.

We love and bond with all the kittens, but when you have a litter (or two) running around with the energy level and destructive potential of Devons, it makes it a little easier to hand them off. In all seriousness, I do miss the kittens when they leave us, but it's part of what we do and we get used to it. It is extremely bittersweet when we send off retired adults to new homes, though. I've had to say goodbye to girls that, with all my heart, I wanted to keep as my own pets. But every adult, just like every kitten, deserves to have an absolutely amazing life where they get spoiled and doted on by a family that best fits their personality (after being spayed/neutered in the case of retired adults). Knowing that I found them that home and that they are happy in it makes it worthwhile, because it is all about them.

We've gotten a few more cats over the years, but otherwise we haven't gotten any bigger, and all our cats still occupy our house with us. We do have a decent-sized online following now, and I easily have ten to twenty preapproved families waiting for kittens at any given time. Even with more cats, we don't have more litters than we did a decade ago because they are a lot of work. Having a cattery is a hobby for us; both my husband and I work full-time outside the home and neither of us desire to grow the cattery beyond its current size. It's also an expensive hobby, which helps with self-limiting any ideas of expansion; we can easily spend a thousand dollars a month on food and litter alone when we have a couple litters of kittens in the house.

I love meeting the families who adopt the cats in person whenever possible! As much as I get out of meeting the family, they get to see our home and our cats and how they all interact with each other and with us, which is just as important. It's also so much fun getting to see their faces light up when they meet their new kitty. I've been fortunate that we've never had a bad experience with having a family over. I do remember a lot of amazing families who have come over during the years: a family with adorable twins with cat allergies who didn't have a reaction to ours and were able to get a cat from us; a few local families who would come over every week or two to play with their babies as they grew; the handful of families who have driven from surrounding states and as far north as Canada; and even the times where I've been a courier and flown or driven a kitten to his or her family.

There is definitely room for both breeding cats and for cats to be rescued, and there's no reason why people can't buy and rescue. Prior to having Devons, all of my cats were free kittens or from shelters. But there are reasons many people want a specific breed of cat (temperament, allergies, etc.), and there's no guarantee you'll get that with a rescue cat. Ironically, I've seen people condemn breeders for breeding in one breath, and in the next state that they've been looking for *X* breed of cat to rescue. It would be a horrible loss to humanity if all these amazing breeds of cats did not exist because some people feel there shouldn't be breeders. Over the years, I've noticed there are a lot of misconceptions about breeders, and many times people tend to lump every type of breeder together because they don't know the differences. There are mills—these are people who don't care about the breed or the animals, just about turning a profit—and backyard breeders who do a disservice to the breed because they often have little knowledge about the breed and are in it for profit as well. But hobby breeders, breeders who show their cats, even who do it on a large scale, are ever working toward the health, temperament, and ideal standard of their chosen breed. We are not overproducing or populating animal shelters, and we are here to support our families and cats for their entire lives.

Naomi Kolb is the owner of Montana Devons, a small TICA, CFA, and ACFA registered family cattery located in Missoula, Montana.

Killer

EMMA STRAUB

Yesterday, Killer, my thirteen-year-old cat, went to the vet to have her snaggletooth removed. It was horribly infected, and had been for quite some time, but we'd put off the procedure because, as our five-year-old put it, it was the main thing on her face. Marilyn Monroe's beauty mark. Anna Wintour's bangs. Killer's tooth had style. We agreed it was a shame to see it go.

When I took Killer to the vet before her procedure, I described Killer, as I often do, as the greatest cat in the world. "You must hear that all the time," I said to the vet, assuming that every pet parent is pretty much like any human parent, filled with the need for other people to recognize the beauty and wondrousness of their small creatures. "No," the vet told me. "I really don't hear it that much." I thought of Killer's sister, deceased now for two years—a beautiful yowler who peed on the couch—and understood what she meant.

Don't worry, the cat does not die in this essay.

It was a romantic comedy from the start—I was looking for an orange cat. Because I grew up in the 1980s—home to both Heathcliff and Garfield—I spent my childhood pining for an orange cat. I drew orange cats all the time. I made three-dimensional orange cats stuffed with crumpled newspaper. I craved an orange cat of my own. Twenty years later, my boyfriend and I moved in together, and it was time.

I found a batch of orange rescue kittens on Petfinder, the guiltless pornography website for the besotted cuddlers among us. I wrote the woman with the orange kittens and we made a date to meet at her apartment in the East Village. My boyfriend and I went up in the elevator, and as soon as we got off, we could smell which direction the cats lived. The woman hurried out of a door at the end of the hall, and opened the door to a neighboring apartment, which was spotless and Lysol-clean, what to my 2018 eye looks like an Airbnb hustle, but to my 2004 eye just looked weird. She then went back to Planet Cat and returned with a cardboard box full of orange cats. I lifted one small specimen up and put it on my lap, where it stayed, immobilized and purring. I thought the cat (whom we brought home and named Gravyboat) was a lovebug before I realized that the immobilized purring indicated pure, paralyzed fear. But then the woman went back and returned with still another box of cats, and out of this one sprang a tiny black kitten that immediately scampered onto our shoulders to shower us with kisses. This was our meet cute. This was our Killer. We were Mount Everest and she was our intrepid mountain climber. This was love.

Lo these many years later, Killer still does this with every human who walks into our house, much to the chagrin of my mother-in-law and all other allergic and/or cat-phobic visitors. She jumps onto laps and shoulders, she purrs, she nudges chins and cheeks with her damp little velvet nose. We're not gifted cat-tamers by any means—Killer was born with a surfeit of love. Unlike with human children, I claim no influence. Even the irritating things Killer does are in service of this abundance—when she paces on my pillow while I'm trying to fall asleep, when she runs down the stairs with me, her slim black body slipping in between my feet—because she is a people cat, and people cats want to be with their people.

When my husband returned from the vet with Killer, her eight-pound body sleepy, sad, and snuggled into the pink towel on the bottom of her carrier, I picked her up and held her against me. She's now the size of my children when they were newborns, and smaller than she was in her prime. In addition to her signature snaggletooth, the vet had removed three other rotten scoundrels,

leaving Killer with a grand total of two teeth, sitting in opposite corners of her mouth. Killer hid under the bed for two days.

Just when I had started to worry that we'd killed our Killer, in spirit if not in body, she emerged from under the bed. She leaped onto our shoulders. She asked for breakfast twice. At night, she turned around and around until she finally fell asleep in the crook of my arm, right next to my face, right where she belongs.

What is a cat? An aloof bundle of fluff, a standoffish stray, a peeved princess, a scratcher, a biter. Our Killer is none of those things. Our Killer is an ancient Egyptian goddess. Whenever Killer meets her end, some dark day in the future, the seas will roil and the heavens will cloud, at least outside our windows. We are lucky to have her now. The snaggletooth was just an accessory. Who needs to gild a lily?

Emma Straub is the best-selling author of books including *Modern Lovers* and *The Vacationers*. She is the owner of Brooklyn's Books Are Magic bookstore.

Black Cats

Throughout much of Western history, black cats have been associated with misfortune and witchcraft. We keep these beliefs alive annually through Halloween decorations and persistent superstitions. But it's not all bad for the black cat. In England, it is believed that a black cat crossing your path is good luck, or a black cat given to a bride on her wedding day will bring good fortune. In Scotland, the arrival of a black cat at your home signals prosperity, and in Japan, a single woman who owns a black cat is thought to attract more suitors.

On Cats and Motherhood

AN INTERVIEW WITH LATONYA YVETTE

Between running her lifestyle website full-time, working as a stylist, promoting her new book, and chasing her two children, River and Oak, and two kittens, Langston and St. James, around her Clinton Hill, Brooklyn apartment, LaTonya Yvette is certifiably busy. Her self-titled blog focuses on family, style, design, and well-being, and Yvette is able to share tips for putting together effortless winter outfits in one post, and write candidly about learning to love her body postpartum in the next. The blog led to her first book, *Woman of Color*, a part memoir, part-lifestyle guide. I talked with Yvette about how the recent addition of cats has changed life at home for her and her kids.

Yvette: I'm a Brooklyn native, and the street cats in my city are unavoidable. It's funny, though, because I never thought of them as "pets." I see them as part of the community. A dog is a pet. A cat is a cat. I think that's especially true for New York because they walk past you like they're your neighbor, or they walk in and out of the bodega, or sit on the counter as you grab your candy.

Now I have my own cats who are pets. I recently adopted two kittens: Langston, who is black and white, and St. James, who is a broken mackerel tabby with a Bengal feel. They are brothers from the same litter, but I am not fully convinced they have the same dad. They are both so different! It's funny, because I did not grow up with pets, and having kittens has *been an experience*. I love them so much. *So much.* But they are also a pain in certain ways I didn't antic-ipate. Which is also fine, and part of being a parent—both a parent of children and a pet parent.

The cats are both so incredibly obsessed with my children and have grown to be boundaryless with strangers because my kids are all over them. I've heard so much about cats having certain areas where they don't want to be touched, or weird habits, but despite their unique personalities they both are totally open and people friendly. They let you pet them anywhere and hold them like babies.

Langston is super sweet—you will *never* see his claws—and is a bit silly in ridiculous ways. He snores and you can hear him breathing from the next room. And, no, apparently he does not have any issues. He is just a bit like an old man.

St. James is extra. Everything he does is *so* extra. But he's also extremely smart and on top of everything. He cries at my door whenever I am working or have company and am hiding from him a bit, because apparently he never gets enough pets. He plays hard, but at the same time *loves* so hard. He will come sniff you and then wrap his tail around you. He even greets me at the door when I walk in! The cat sitters love him because he's so affectionate.

For me, the cats were also a test of my own boundaries and still are. I have always had odd impostor feelings with the idea of home, and I've needed controlled environments. The cats have shifted my anxieties about home because they don't exist within that world. They don't sit when I say sit, and they don't chill while I'm often chill (though I know that may happen as they get older). They have helped me heal a bit when it comes to my own relationship with home. The kids have done that in their own way, of course, but I've also mothered with myself in mind, which made it easier to have kids.

But that being said, whenever I have a bad day, somehow my cats *do* know how to chill and just *force* me to sit by lying on me, burying their bodies into mine, begging for pets, and eventually falling asleep. They force me to kind of slow down when I need it the most.

A lot of my children's learning with the cats has already taken place, thankfully. It initially started with learning that cats aren't people and have their own language. We have to listen to

their language and we have to respect their language, just as we want people to respect ours. After a few scratches early on, my son realized he couldn't just do whatever he wanted and that cats need space and will let you know when they're afraid, tired, or experiencing another emotion. It's been really important.

For the long haul, I'm invested in my kids having a sense of responsibility with the cats. But more importantly, I love that there's this extension of family with them as well. We are all in love with them, miss them when we're away, and love coming home to them.

LaTonya Yvette is a Brooklyn, New York–born stylist, writer, and blogger. Her first book, *Woman of Color*, is part memoir, part-lifestyle guide.

Why Do Cats Always Land on Their Feet?

It's complicated. Cats' bodies are small and light and they have an innate sense of balance and direction. They also have far more bones in their bodies than we do, making them extremely flexible. Their spines have more vertebrae, too, enabling them to twist their bodies back into an upright position as they fall. Cats are born with this "righting reflex," and most have it down by the time they're seven weeks old.

Small Thoughts on Being a Dog Lady

AIDY BRYANT

Hello. I am a Dog Lady. Not to be confused with a Dog Person. One of those golden retriever people, you know them, strapping on their hiking boots to hoof around with their big strong dog to point and look at big rocks, a.k.a. mountains. Nay, I am a Dog Lady, a woman who is meant to sit on an elaborate cushion in an ornate housecoat eating small buttery cookies. Next to me there is a smaller more ornate cushion where my fat and rude small dog rests. I have spent many a rainy day in my apartment with my "mean to everyone else" terrier-poodle-rat mix and it is the ultimate experience in pet ownership. I love to stare at his pink belly, smell his dirty feet, and give him a head massage so deep and intimate that his eyes close like a man exhausted by his long day's work at a factory. Hour after hour I have wondered why anyone would want any other kind of companion. And so I submit to you, reader, as an act of hostility, a collection of small thoughts as to why dogs are superior. Come at me.

1. There have been many great showbiz dogs! Lassie, Eddie from *Frasier*, Wishbone, that dog that went to the Oscars for that silent film? And can you even name one famous cat actor? Sure, you say, Salem from *Sabrina the Teenage Witch*, but I'm sorry, more than half of that cat's work was done by an animatronics cat.
2. I relate to dogs as workers. Service dogs, police dogs, those weird nurse dogs with little barrels around their necks—they just want to help. They don't have hands, but they still make it work. I have never seen a cat do a day of work in its goddamned life.
3. Have you ever seen a dog do a full body roll on very green grass? It is pure art.

4. My family did have a cat. She was a black cat with green eyes and her name was "H." Named by my parents for her description as a "Hell Cat" because she behaved very badly and I assume because she worshipped Satan as her god. Most of my memories of "H" are her walking through the room I was in to get to a different room where I wasn't, or her yowling in a way that I was very good at mimicking.

5. Cats are so often villains and I am easily swayed by media. Examples: *Lady and The Tramp*, *The Smurfs*, and all films starring mice.

6. Mice are cute.

7. I enjoy eating peanut butter, chicken, and trash. I do not eat fish, milk, or fancy feasts.

8. A friend of mine once allowed me to stay at her apartment in Los Angeles and in return I was to care for her two cats. Her two extremely ill and hauntingly old cats. To best sum it up for you, I would describe it in a few words: harrowing, medication, turd heavy, sleeplessness, ghoulish.

9. Cats are formal. Dogs are casual. Cats are Mr. and Mrs. Dogs are "Heyyyyy bud!" Cats are prissy. Dogs are clumsy. Cats are tricksters. Dogs are easily tricked.

10. Dogs are funnier. Though they are not aware of it, they are dumb in all the right ways. Note: I can acknowledge that cats have their own better private sense of humor that sustains them. I have certainly felt cats laugh at me before and felt that I was not in on the joke. Also, cats have funnier toys.

11. I still can't wrap my head around a litter box. So much equipment for piss and shit.
12. Sheepdogs are the bosses of sheep. They are in charge of other animals, which is incredible. Is there a snake that's the boss of a parrot? A turtle that manages a ferret? A hamster that bargains with a lizard?
13. According to a study I read on a pet food website that I did not fact-check and will not even cite here, cat owners are more logical and practical than dog owners. I believe that. I'm stupid like my dog, but I like it that way.

Aidy Bryant is an actor and comedian known for her work on *Saturday Night Live* and her Hulu series *Shrill*.

First Cat
in Space

On October 18, 1963, a former Parisian street cat, Félicette, traveled nearly one hundred miles above the Earth before safely parachuting back home. Few remember her as the first cat in space—they remember the first man, of course, or the first dog, or monkey, or even confuse her with a male cat named Felix! A recent campaign to erect a bronze statue of Félicette in her hometown of Paris will soon "restore a female astronaut's rightful place in history."

On Finding Joy

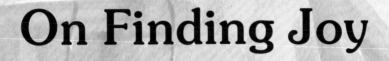

AN INTERVIEW WITH JEN GOTCH

Jen Gotch is fearless. She's not afraid to match a silver sequined jacket with a 1970s floral minidress and record herself dancing in front of the parking garage dumpster before showing up to manage a team of forty at the company she built. If it ends up being a tough day, she's not afraid to cry at work, post a photo of herself crying at work, and then design an airbrush-style T-shirt that says "I Cry at Work" so we can all be in on the joke while feeling a little less alone. It's hard not to feel like Jen Gotch's biggest fan. Gotch is the chief creative officer of ban.do, a Los Angeles–based lifestyle, accessory, and apparel company that's been growing in leaps and bounds since she founded it with a friend in 2008. Ban.do's products range from practical yet fun to silly: there are floral luggage tags, sequined phone cases, disco ball party cups, and even an ice cream cone–shaped lamp. As an illustrator for ban.do over the years I've drawn patterns of girls, beauty products, summer accessories, and of course, plenty of cats.

Several years ago I finally met Gotch in person. The lobby of ban.do's expansive office was filled with disco balls, pink streamers, and blown-up pool floaties, yet still felt sparse and professional. They had just moved in and Gotch was apologetic about the mess—albeit the most fun, glittery mess. I was fairly self-conscious to be in the presence of a woman whom I revered from afar and I remember all the details of what I wore (tattered thrift-store dress souped up by my most expensive Rachel Comey sweater), what I ordered at lunch (ahi tuna salad), and what I said. But the thing about Gotch is, it really didn't matter! She'll talk to anyone and tell them anything. Her constant joking and laughter make you instant friends.

I caught up with Gotch again to ask her about her cat, Gertie, her public journey with mental health, and all those fun products she's dreaming up for ban.do, including maybe, maybe a cat-shaped speaker.

Gotch: I've been a cat person most of my life. I grew up with cats. I didn't just not understand dogs, I was *anti*-dog. And then I met Philip. *No way*, I thought. And then he wiggled his way into our lives.

Suddenly, I was wondering, *why would you ever have a cat?* Friends who were there during that transition in my life would make fun of me because I'd go around cooing, *ooh what's your dog's name?* I went full-fledged to the other side.

My ex-husband Andrew worked at Guess at their big campus in downtown Los Angeles. There were a lot of strays downtown, and he loves cats so he was always around them. One of the cats had a litter of kittens and put them down in the sewer to protect them. He went back to the office in the middle of the night on a rescue mission and came home with a box of kittens around three weeks old. Right around Christmastime we had six kittens in our house. We were bottle-feeding them and living the best life. We had a New Year's Eve party where people just came and sat by the fire and held kittens. It was the best New Year's ever. Our dog Philip would guard the kittens, and he wasn't aggressive with them at all. We had no intention of keeping any of them, but Philip took a particular liking to Gertie, and we began to think how it would be cool to have a dog and a cat since we were both cat people prior. The other kittens all got adopted out to friends.

Andrew ended up saving two more litters, and he also trapped the mother at one point to get her fixed. We ended up having sixteen or eighteen kittens come through the house that year and then we fostered them all out. We kept the kittens in the guest room, and I was in there with them every day, cleaning and feeding them. They crawl all over you and get in your pockets and they're so cute. There's nothing cuter than a kitten—there really isn't. By the end, I couldn't do it anymore. There were times when I fantasized about keeping them all. I would get so attached to them and then I would just cry—I was so sad. I would have to leave when my friends would come to take them. My friends! I wasn't giving them to strangers! After I declared no more, we still ended up with one last kitten, an abandoned runt who was two weeks old. And after that, I *really* couldn't take it anymore. It was too hard. It was a great experience, a really fun period in my life, but it was too emotional for me.

I suffered from a myriad of mental health issues even as a child. I was born in 1971, so it wasn't exactly "the olden times," but there was really no mental health awareness unless it was very overt. At twenty-three I was misdiagnosed with depression and put on medication. Soon after, I moved out to California and went into therapy. I was really against therapy growing up because my mom did it, and anything my mom did I wanted to do the opposite! But I got to California, and it was a cool thing! For the next eight years or so there was a professional guiding me through my symptoms and helping me understand what was going on. Growing up at the same time was also a big factor. What's a job?! Things like that. I was diagnosed with ADD and depression and put on medication for both. The whole time, I had bipolar disorder and no one knew it—it's very commonly misdiagnosed. The medications I was taking made it worse. With the correct diagnosis we were quickly able to get me on the right protocol as far as medications go. I was miraculously fine from that point on, relatively speaking. It doesn't mean I don't have those issues anymore, but it's completely managed. Now, sixteen years later I know it all very well. It went from being an unknown thing to recognizing, learning, experiencing, troubleshooting, and management.

I never felt like my struggles with mental health were strange or embarrassing. In this way, my relationship to it is different from most people. I don't know why—it could be that my therapist made me feel really comfortable, or there was a part of me that liked having something wrong with me that I could name and identify.

In the last several years since Andrew left, I've had a lot of time to focus on my feelings and work through grief and I've gained more insight than ever before. Sharing this on Instagram just made sense to me. At ban.do some of the girls started calling me a mental health advocate. No, nope! It makes it sound like there was a business plan! I'm just a person who loves to give advice and loves to take

my life experience and share it to help other people. Social media or not, that's how I operate. As I felt like I was gaining traction and getting through to people, I leaned into it more. I respond very well to positive feedback!

Until Gertie, I've only had cats that were neutral or lap cats. Gertie is my first evil cat. She's definitely sweetening up as she gets older but she will also straight up try to murder you. She's wild; I let her become an outdoor cat six months ago and it's really changed our relationship. I've never had an outdoor cat, and I had a lot of anxiety about letting her out, but last year for me was about working through my anxieties because enough was enough. My anxious fantasies were taking up too much time. But Gertie loves it, and we're friends now.

Phil is definitely an emotional support animal. He's like me: he's so sensitive to energy and vibe and mood. He knows when I'm upset—he just knows. The tactile nature of having pets and being able to literally pet them is sometimes enough to calm you down. Any warmth from another living thing especially when you live alone is very comforting. Certainly during the winter there are a lot of family huddles between me and the two of them on the bed. Since Andrew has left, Gertie will surprise me and get on my chest if I'm lying in bed. Phil was also trained from an early age to love hugs and so sometimes I'll sit and hug him when I don't feel good. So sad. Forty-seven-year-old refuses to be a cat lady but hugs pets all the time when she's sad. I use a weighted blanket to help with anxiety, and when it got really bad for me I would get under it and then put treats on top to try to get both of them to lay on top of it. I could take another thirty pounds in addition to the twenty-five-pound blanket.

Last year at ban.do we introduced two nameplate neck-laces that said "Anxiety" and "Depression." They were a step toward reducing the stigma around mental health, and I hoped they could also serve as a conversation starter for people to be more open about what's going on in their minds. I did a lot of soul-searching after launching the necklaces because I felt like we really popped a bubble there, and there was an opportunity to connect my personal mission to the brand. The concept of ban.do had been reduced to just "we're fun!" because it's very digestible. We're not a philan-thropic effort, we're a consumer products company, but we want to help people. We made this conscious pivot because we are in people's lives. When I think about what we're designing and why we're doing it, and why we're painstaking in our process, there's a larger reason behind it. Ban.do is aiming to help people feel their best, do their best, be their best, and encourage them. Learning the difference between being happy and conditional happiness and what joy can actually mean is so big and important and we are always working toward that.

Not surprisingly, cats are a big part of that, too! People love cats! We tried to do a cat speaker a while back but we could not get the pricing right on it. I still talk about it to this day. I had one of those vintage white ceramic cats that you can get at a swap meet, and I would always joke that it was my office pet, when we didn't allow living pets in our office. I dreamed that there was an audio speaker inside of it! There are a lot of similar cat products that never made it through, but we've always been into cats in surface design and as an icon because they evoke joy.

It's a weird time to operate in the world, to have a business and especially to sell things. People are trying to figure out what their worldview is, and I know for me it can be confusing because I want to have an impact on people's lives. I'm a very tactile person—I like *things*. That is in the ethos of ban.do, but sometimes I wonder if this is really doing anything. This feels like a common question that anyone who is on the creative end rather than the business end thinks about. It's not as deep as a moral dilemma, but I think as long as people are still happy and expressing that happiness due to some-thing we produce, it feels like a good thing.

Jen Gotch is the founder and chief creative officer of ban.do, a Los Angeles–based lifestyle brand.

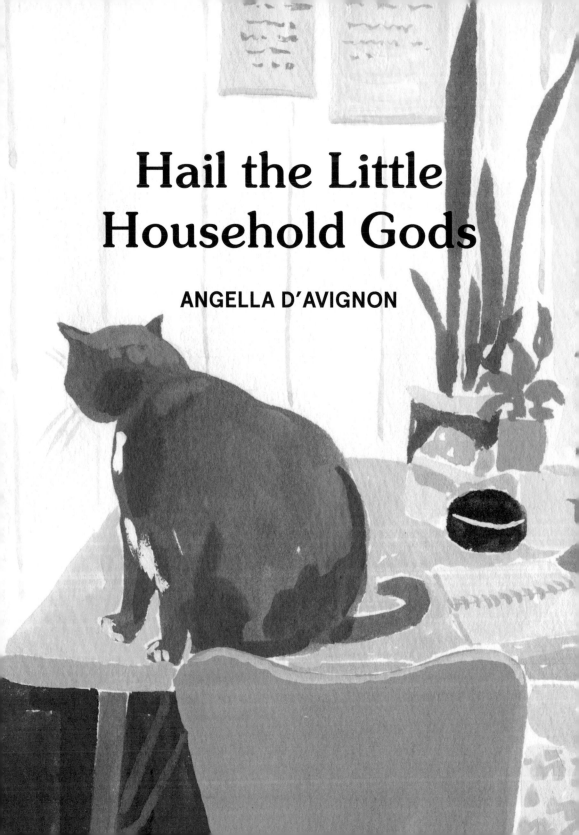

Hail the Little Household Gods

ANGELLA D'AVIGNON

> **"I love cats because I enjoy my home; and little by little,
> they become its visible soul."**
> —Jean Cocteau

I learned from the best: as a career cat woman, my Grandmama always had a cat puttering around each of her elegant homes, from her loft apartment in a former typewriter factory in Chicago to the mattress store she owned named Bed Time where cats slept in the window, to the nooks and crannies of her jewel box bungalows in California where I grew up. Like Grandmama, her cats were always chic, roaming through her various abodes like ancient queens on palatial grounds.

Before the beautiful apartments, though, Grandmama lived a nomadic life. As a single mom, she moved my dad, my two aunts, and all three of their cats from California to Nebraska in the early 1960s. One of them, Tiger, whom Grandmama describes as very laid-back, caught a bad case of carsickness. On their way out of California, they stopped at an artichoke farm. The farmer was told that Tiger was "a real great mouser"; the farmer's daughter ended up adopting her. "I didn't know I was going to be sad until I had to hand her over," Grandmama told me. She had burst into tears when she'd reached back into the van to grab Tiger, the kids bawling along with her all the way to the state line. Crying in the car, hands on the steering wheel, staring down the road at an uncertain future is a posture I found myself holding throughout the years my cat Lyra lived with and without me.

=^-^=

In the comments section of a website where I sourced a Frank O'Hara poem about his beloved tabby cat, Cantata, an anonymous poster wrote: "Hail the little household gods!" Cats, for all their attitude and snarl, are domestic talismans. They're what Jean Cocteau, the French poet and filmmaker who started the Friends Cat Club in Paris during the twentieth century, called the "visible souls" of the home. If this is true, then my cat, an eleven-year-old, gray-and-white tuxedo named Lyra, has been my literal soul mate during the ten apartments I've had since I was twenty-one.

My mother, who is allergic to cats, is fond of repeating my maxim regarding Lyra: "I don't love cats, I love *one* cat." But eventually, the love of one cat turned me into a cat person against my will: I unfailingly genuflect to pet the bodega cat, I ceremoniously offer the back of my hand to an inquisitive neighborhood feline. In other people's homes, I am drawn helplessly to their cats peeking from behind doorways or slinking underfoot. Historically, cats are constant companions to writers. Cats are luxurious—soft, languid, and secretive, they affect an air of posh erudition. Writing is essentially a sophisticated way to be a layabout; cats turn any surface they deign to sit on into a chaise longue glamorous enough for a movie star. When asked why there seems to be a special kinship between writers and cats, science fiction writer Ursula K. Le Guin wondered, "Maybe because writers don't want to have to stop writing and walk the dog?"

As homebodies, cats and writers make natural housemates. Home is where I work and home is where Lyra is.

For me (and Jean Cocteau), cats are synonymous with the notion of home. In the twelve years I've owned Lyra (my longest relationship to date), we've suffered periods of forced separation due to lean budgets or brutish landlords with inflexible pet policies. During those lonely times (at least for me), Lyra luxuriated at my grandmama's condo, where she had an entire room to herself, complete with a high-rise "cat condo" (as Grandmama called it, a glorified standard carpet tower from the pet store), a can or two of wet food a day (Lyra gained considerable weight, but it's a Grandmama's prerogative to feed a grandchild), and a full bed's worth of stuffed animals to lounge with. She was spoiled, fat, and happy as all cats are intended to be. No matter where I lived, though, Lyra was the spirit of that particular apartment or room, whether or not she was present.

The tumult of my twenties meant I moved around a lot; Lyra gamely came along. There was my very first apartment in San Diego on Twenty-Third Street, where my neighbor gifted us with enough plants to fill my studio with greenery. I became myself in this apartment and Lyra grew alongside me. At a shared house nicknamed F Street for its constant atmosphere of fun, my roommates and I enjoyed cooking together and often sunbathed on the roof, baffling Lyra as to how we had found her spot. She used to salute me from the roof or walk me to the top of the hill when I left for work on my bike. I was twenty-four. To escape a bad breakup, I moved to a shitty apartment on Park Avenue where I rebuilt my life with Salvation Army furniture and wrapped kerchiefs around Lyra's neck to create a festive feeling that just wasn't there. Another apartment was in a building that used to be a hotel—large, blocky, and painted the color of chewed gum. At the time, I was so broke I sold my hair for money. But I was finally doing something with my life by writing and working at museums. A neighbor gave us a white, shaggy wool rug, and Lyra loved it so much that when my friend house-sat he could brush enough cat hair out of it to make a ball of gray fuzz the size of his hand.

Lyra's favorite house was affectionately called the Womansion, because it was a hollowed-out Victorian with a sinking foundation filled with women on any given day. It was lopsided, but it also had big rooms and a balcony. Lyra used to sit on the balcony ledge while we enjoyed the breeze. We had a French neighbor who would watch her from his window and would come over to tell us if "Laura" was stuck. "How's that Laura?" he would ask us at the market next door. I never corrected him. Lyra and I have moved with U-Hauls, borrowed trucks, and with my ancient Volvo stuffed to the

gills with my plants, books, and just enough breathing room for Lyra's carry bag.

When roommates invariably ask, "Wouldn't it be cute if Lyra could talk?" I shake my head in disagreement. She keeps all my secrets; within the soft gray fur of her body is the spirit of every house I have lived in since my twenties, the memory of every ex-boyfriend, every hangover and bad decision, every triumph and failure. She even carries the heartache of friends who came over to cry in my room: Lyra always knew who needed comfort.

I once lost Lyra in the rain while moving with an Astro van. I was beside myself in a bank parking lot, sopping wet, crouching with muddy sneakers to look underneath each parked car. My dad joined me, equally stressed, as we wandered the asphalt straining to hear her meow or yelp against the din of a thunderstorm. We finally found her a half hour later, pissed off and huddled near the back door of a bar, tucked behind a rain gutter and caked in mud. Happy and soaked to the bone, I squeezed Lyra and drove the ten miles to my new house covered in mud and crying with Lyra wrapped in a towel on my lap.

Women chasing their cats is a genre of its own. In that parking lot, I sobbed like Holly Golightly in *Breakfast at Tiffany's* shuffling through an alley full of garbage. And how many times have I flung open the screen door yelling my cat's name into the dark, stumbling through the neighborhood like Mary Gaitskill in her short story "Lost Cat," only to discover Lyra had been hiding under my bed all along? I have also been Natasha Lyonne in *Russian Doll*, who sputters to a stranger in the park, "Life is a fucking nightmare, right? Being a person is a fucking nightmare. And that is why I love this little fucking guy." She then reaches out and takes her cat, Oatmeal, whom she's been chasing through nine plus lives of her own as she (spoiler alert) repeatedly dies on-screen. Like Holly, Mary, and Natasha, I am lost without my cat; without her the fabric of my idea of home frays.

I'm not just chasing my pet, I'm chasing what makes my house feel like home, the creature without whom I am incomplete, pacing the room mindlessly, wondering where my center went. I'm lost without Lyra; finding her is finding home and finding myself in it.

Angella d'Avignon is a writer and reporter from Southern California now based in New York. She writes art criticism, narrative non-fiction, and profiles on people she finds fascinating.

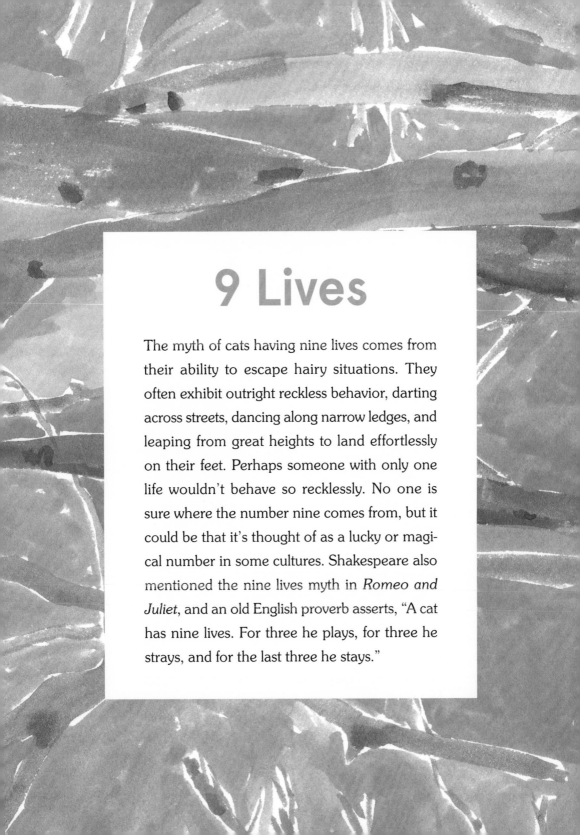

9 Lives

The myth of cats having nine lives comes from their ability to escape hairy situations. They often exhibit outright reckless behavior, darting across streets, dancing along narrow ledges, and leaping from great heights to land effortlessly on their feet. Perhaps someone with only one life wouldn't behave so recklessly. No one is sure where the number nine comes from, but it could be that it's thought of as a lucky or magical number in some cultures. Shakespeare also mentioned the nine lives myth in *Romeo and Juliet*, and an old English proverb asserts, "A cat has nine lives. For three he plays, for three he strays, and for the last three he stays."

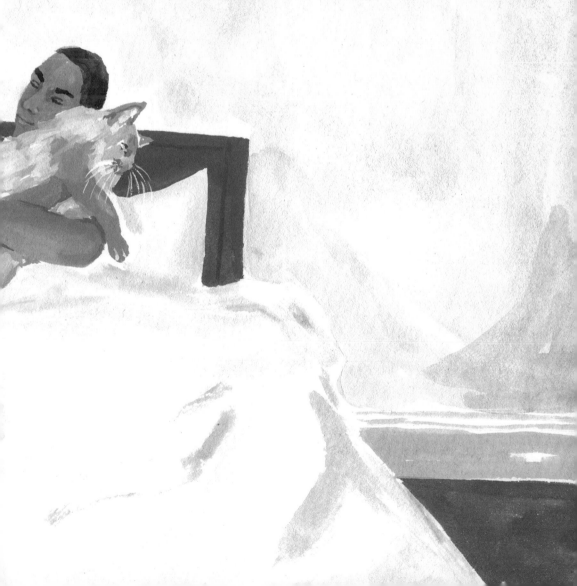

On Cats and Therapy

AN INTERVIEW WITH NATALIE ENRIGHT

When Natalie Enright brought home Lou, a fluffy Siberian kitten, six years ago, I couldn't help but notice she was doing cat lady a little differently. For one, she and her husband were quite allergic, and Lou was anything but hairless. And two, she somehow got him to put on a leash and hop inside their VW Westfalia for weekend camping trips around the Bay Area. Seeing them, I began to question whether I, a lifelong bearer of a stuffy nose and former dog owner, could have a cat of my own.

Enright lives in San Francisco where she works at the public library. I talked to Enright about adding Lou to her family.

Enright: I was first diagnosed with multiple sclerosis when I was working at a university in San Diego. I was at a desk mostly, staring at a screen. One day I couldn't see the computer screen very well. I had always had twenty-twenty vision. But suddenly everywhere I looked was blurred and darker in one eye. At the same time my hands and feet were always numb. I danced ballet for years. I never had problems with balance, but around this same time I would also stumble or lose my balance when I walked. I didn't even know all of these symptoms were related or that it was the result of multiple sclerosis. My first thought was to see an optometrist and have my eyes checked. I was sure I just needed glasses, but that wasn't the case. I was quickly referred from one specialist to another until I met with a neurologist. I had an MRI and several other tests. When they looked at the MRI scans of my brain and spinal cord, they discovered several significant lesions. We all have nerve cells in our brain and spinal cord. My immune system attacks the covering of these cells to create lesions. This damages communication in my nervous system. MS affects people differently, but the damage can result in physical, mental, and even psychiatric challenges. I have definitely experienced all of these challenges at different times and with different severity in the almost nine years I have had MS.

Some days I *almost* feel like I did before I was diagnosed.

I'm not always hyperaware of what's slowly (but sometimes rapidly) happening to my body. I feel that peace most when my body allows me to do what I want to do. I feel this when I can sit in meditation comfortably without pain or a busy brain, or when I have the energy to hike or stroll around the city without my legs trembling or stiffening up. But then there are days when I'm completely aware that I have an autoimmune disease. It expresses itself in different ways. Sometimes it's pain. Other times walking across my apartment is difficult and I have to stay in bed for long periods of time or else use a cane. I struggle with chronic fatigue and migraines. The worst is how susceptible I am to infections. Working at a public library, someone is always sick. I love my job, but that is an aspect of the work that I had to consider when choosing this career. My immune system is so busy attacking my brain and spinal cord that it's not always protecting me from illness. I have to be vigilant about my health. The things I do are things we could all benefit from: stress management, exercise, rest, healthy diet, etc., but now there is no negotiating. Every day I have to be mindful of managing my stress and ensuring I am giving my body what it needs—nourishment or rest—so that I can enjoy those days when I'm able to do what I want.

After I was diagnosed I began my treatment through the MS Center. My neurologist explained my diagnosis, and different medications I would take. Looking back, it was very overwhelming. It felt like I was constantly at the hospital receiving bad news. I was fortunate to have the support of my husband, my family, and my friends. The doctors talked to me about other resources beyond just taking medicine. One of those resources were support groups to engage with other people who were living with MS. I researched different options. Through my search I heard over and over again the benefits of pets for people who are living with chronic illnesses.

My husband and I are both allergic to cats, but I didn't ever think of us as dog people because of our lifestyle. We have a tiny apartment in the city and it feels unfair to have a dog. I still liked cats even though I was allergic. I was in school in Paris one summer, and there was this guy that would come to the café right by the apartment I was staying in, and he had a cat on a leash. They would go there and just chill every morning. It got me thinking having a cat like that would be amazing.

Through a support group for multiple sclerosis, I met a woman who also had an autoimmune disease, and she had Lou, his littermates, and his parents. Her name was, perfectly, Kitty. She was really gracious with sharing her story and what worked for her. When she described how living with cats helped as therapy companions it really piqued my interest. Her cats were Siberians, and they were supposedly hypoallergenic. I explained that I was allergic, and she said, *maybe you can just come to my house and see if it affects you at all.*

I'm originally from Kenya. I have lived around (wild) animals but never in my home. I didn't know the first thing about taking care of an animal. I completely nerded out online and at the library checking out books about living with cats and taking care of them. Kitty was great about answering all of my questions, too. She let us come to her home and see where Lou would be until we could take him home with us. She lived in the Berkeley Hills in a large old house with a jungle of plants and trees around and inside her home. It was lovely. The cats were napping on shelves and furniture in her large living room. The cats were all well socialized and would come up to you and rub their head on your leg and let you pet them. I felt comfortable in her home. I didn't sneeze once, and neither did James.

The kittens were all healthy and energetic. Lou was this fluffy little cotton ball when we first saw him. Kitty took such good care of Lou and his littermates, which helped his transition into our home. She shared her raw food recipe that she gave her cats, and we kept him on a raw meat diet.

It didn't take long for him to settle into our apartment and warm up to us, and that made it easier to take him outside with us. I wouldn't call him an "adventure cat"; he's more like a "kitty of

leisure in the great outdoors." When we take him camping with us, he enjoys exploring the immediate area and pouncing on insects. But then he finds a grassy area in the sun or fallen branch to nap on until it's time to eat. He enjoys going outside and getting out of the city as much as we do. Being able to watch him enjoy nature with us makes me happy. It's my way of thanking him for when he sits next to me when I'm sick in bed. My husband and I often joke that Lou is my live-in nurse. He'll lie next to me, purr, and chill when I'm in pain. It helps me relax and not panic. And that's big with MS. Stress can easily trigger attacks or "relapses." The symptoms of those relapses can be temporary or permanent. Lou helps me relax.

I should also add that my only connection with Lou is not when he sits with me when I'm ill in bed. He has quite the personality.

He is pretty vocal, and it's not unusual for him to respond to us with a meow that makes me think he understands. Some cats seem aloof when they're called, and that is fine, but Lou will come running to you when you call his name, even if he's in another room. He greets us at the door when we come home. He also seems to enjoy being in the same room with everyone. Whether we're cooking in the kitchen, reading in the living room, or watching movies in bed, Lou will always come sit with us. If my husband is fixing something in our place, Lou will sit next to his toolbox until he's done. And he's playful. He'll retrieve a crumpled piece of paper if you throw it and he loves to chase an old wine cork on the hardwood floor.

We have a small patio that he can access safely on his own. I enjoy peeking out the window and seeing him patrol his domain. He looks very regal and confident. It makes me think that he's not completely domesticated and his natural instincts are still very present. I love that about Lou.

Natalie Enright has a Master of Library and Information Science. She lives in San Francisco where she works for the San Francisco Public Library.

Cat-Eye Makeup

Winged and kohl-rimmed eyes first bring to mind Cleopatra, the ancient Egyptian ruler commonly credited with kicking off the trend. In those times, the makeup was composed of various minerals, including malachite and copper ore, ground and mixed with oil or fat to form a cream. The introduction of liquid eyeliner in the 1950s propelled the look into modern times. In the '60s, Italian actress Sophia Loren brought her glamorous cat eye to Hollywood, and supermodel Twiggy later added a mod spin with chunky eyelashes and color-blocked eye shadow. In more recent years, the singer Amy Winehouse was known for painting on an extra-bold swoosh until her untimely death in 2011.

Familiar

RAWAAN ALKHATIB

Sunset, and a very small black cat appears.

"This cat," said my father, "is obviously a djinni."

"It's just a cat," I replied.

"Look at its face!"

"The face of a cat."

"Then why," ominously, "is it looking at me like that?"

The cat did in fact, for all its tininess, possess an air of remarkable unconcern. It frolicked at our feet, very, very charming, as we sweated in the humid Dubai air. Dusk was less a respite from the heat than an absence of sunlight; around us, the air settled to the texture of murky bathwater, trapping the day's warmth so our movements thickened and slowed.

"Can we keep it?" I asked. My parents were playing host to at least a dozen garden cats and one more did not seem like it would make much difference to the weekly tinned sardine budget.

I was at the time living in a tiny box in a distant city with no outdoor space whatsoever and no access to any sort of garden beyond a series of doomed potted plants that I cultivated passionately beneath a weak and crookedly installed grow lamp. If I could not maintain a monstera then what hope did I have of owning a pet? The closest thing to a creature I could claim was an algae-furred marimo, a spherical little moss ball cultivated in a faraway lake. They grow so slowly that the marimo I eventually abandoned, wilting and yellowed, was probably several years old before I got my wastrel clutches on it. A shame. A waste of a good blob.

That the little cat materialized at sunset was only one of the arguments against its remaining a member of the household ménage; it had too friendly and mischievous a face and its tail, which looked less like a feline appendage and more like a bottlebrush or electrified feather boa, wagged like a dog's. It had the demeanor of a witch's familiar. I found the devil-may-care twinkle in its eye deeply appealing; the other members of my family were less convinced.

My parents' garden is an easy place to lose oneself in,

particularly if one is a cat. It is a playground: mulberry trees and lime trees and twining bougainvillea vines in a rainbow of animate petals; a pomegranate tree at the front gate; stands of tiny palm trees that are dwarfed by comically large harvests of dates every summer. There are screen doors to claw and itinerant hoopoes to stalk. Other cats from other neighborhood houses deign to visit, from time to time, to be welcomed or viciously ousted. A large green lawn offers ample room for night creeping and the sort of tactical military moves that cats like to orchestrate at dusk, chasing bugs or ghosts.

A cat is incomprehensible, vague yet pointed, a dainty foot always in another dimension. Even the doofiest of cats harbors secrets. A single, warm, purring bundle that can contort itself into otherworldly pretzels, stretch to double its length or flow through the tiniest of spaces unscathed. No surprise that one could see a cat and think instead it must be a supernatural being.

Signs your cat is, in fact, a djinni:

> It manifests at sunset
> It likes to live in trees
> It can be affectionate or wild
> It is an invisible entity made of smokeless fire
> It is an empty vessel composed of its own ego and intention; it mirrors she who observes it
> It is unpredictable *and* emotional
> Its eyes glow yellow
> It displays discomfort when confronted with straightforward affection
> It is simultaneously repulsed and enchanted by your presence
> It may or may not purr

I have known many cats in my life—Belly, who birthed her kittens beneath my duvet; Pico, who curled up on my tummy as we napped together in the warm summer grass; Zaatoora, with eyes the color of wild thyme and a willfully aloof air. But this cat felt like a fully formed personality, a tiny bundle emitting opinions and prancing about with a clear delight in its own sense of humor. I can't even remember if it did anything—just peered up at us with an expression on its face that was clearly laughter, eyes sparkling. This, my father indicated, was part of its djinni-ness.

Factions developed that night at the dinner table. To keep or not to keep? Should we be sensible, supernatural-fearing hosts or should we just cuddle its tiny adorable face? What if it scared the other cats away from the garden by being magical or also just mean? Some family members expressed discomfort at being asked for their opinions on such an unusual subject; others were noisily certain we would be inviting evil into the home.

Here is a story: a woman leaves her home and moves a great distance into her own private space, building a life of small ritual and routine and shocking her family and friends with her "need" for "independence." She is very lonely and very happy. One day a cat appears in her home, clamoring for milk and attention; simultaneously, the woman realizes she is a witch. Or: a woman's cat disappears and it is only once he is gone that she understands that she is a witch in sore need of her familiar and her friend. Or: witnessing a cat pounce at last upon a doomed dove, the woman realizes that she is a witch. The cat creates itself; the woman becomes a witch. The cat enters the portal. The woman becomes a witch. One morning I woke to an absence of birdsong and light pouring so greenly through the rippling leaves of the neem tree outside my window that I thought I was underwater; I grappled for my conscious mind and in doing so realized that I had no cat and no name for myself and that my home was very far away.

Hidden worlds caw out a persistence; mynah birds orchestrate a dumb conversion. Vines scrape the walls and cats climb roofward and never reach me.

A large garden rusted with palms, dates frizzing into format amid spiked leaves. Fourteen cats stalk a perimeter, moving into and out of the other world. Their tails point to heaven. The minaret sounds the air thickens with hissing. Sand from the interior drifts at my feet. Humid rivulets slide forms onto the window, toward the earth.

Signs your cat may be a witch's familiar and that you, by extension, may in fact be a witch:

> It nuzzles accordingly
> It encourages misbehaviors
> It bewitches the enemy
> It is both spy and companion
> It seeks for blood
> It evinces no interest in the rituals of your daily life

I wanted to keep the cat, but the cat would not be kept. In the morning, it was gone.

≥•≤

Rawaan Alkhatib is a writer, illustrator, and editor who lives in Brooklyn, New York, and was born and raised in Dubai, UAE. She graduated from the Iowa Writers' Workshop in 2011 with an MFA in poetry.

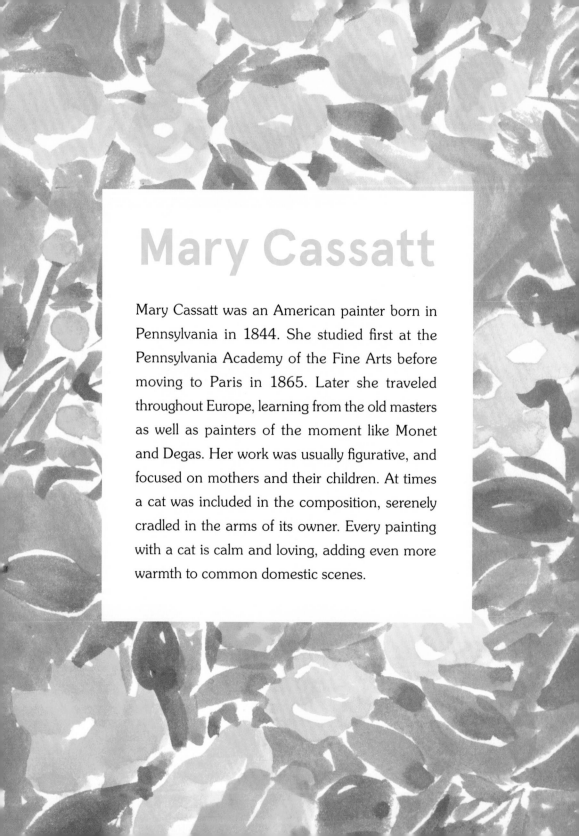

Mary Cassatt

Mary Cassatt was an American painter born in Pennsylvania in 1844. She studied first at the Pennsylvania Academy of the Fine Arts before moving to Paris in 1865. Later she traveled throughout Europe, learning from the old masters as well as painters of the moment like Monet and Degas. Her work was usually figurative, and focused on mothers and their children. At times a cat was included in the composition, serenely cradled in the arms of its owner. Every painting with a cat is calm and loving, adding even more warmth to common domestic scenes.

On Cats in Illustration

AN INTERVIEW WITH KAYE BLEGVAD

The Internet is saturated with cats—cats cuddling with deer, cats improbably squished into tiny boxes, cats with their faces poked through pieces of soft white bread. Most obvious to me, as I scroll through my Instagram feed, are the cats drawn by female illustrators. They're usually in a very pleasing style: graphic swaths of digital color with a texture meant to resemble hand-printing, or wobbly gouache strokes in poppy colors like a modern Matisse. It's become a slightly embarrassing cliché, and one I am very guilty of perpetuating. I wanted to talk about it with my good friend Kaye Blegvad, who's been drawing cats alongside me since day one.

Blegvad is an illustrator from London who currently lives in Brooklyn, New York, with her cat, Eli, a tabby who followed her home one day. She works on many things, including editorial pieces for clients like the *New York Times* and the *New Yorker*, and her own line of jewelry and illustrated products. So much of her work involves cats, from cat-shaped ceramic pitchers and brass wall hooks, to black-and-white cat drawings inked in her sketchbook, to a photo journal of *every* cat she walks past, *ever*.

Blegvad: There is the trope of the crazy cat lady who has a hundred tiny cat figurines and a tote bag printed with cats, but that merchandise has always been around. People loving their animals is not new and neither is wanting stuff with their favorite animals on it. Ancient Egyptians loved cats and made stuff that was not tacky! The difference now is cats became *cool*. It had a bit of a makeover. You hear someone say, "I'm a crazy cat lady," and it's actually a cool young woman. There isn't the same stigma that there used to be. There was a shift that made it slightly ironic or tongue in cheek. Different animals have different moments. In the 1990s everyone had a dolphin tattoo! But cats and dogs have always been classic pets, and for whatever reason cats have been quite popular in the current decade.

There are painters who have done beautiful, interesting pictures that just happen to be of cats, like Mary Fedden, who painted a ton of English seaside cats. It's more than the sum of its parts. In illustration, it's really easy to draw a symbol that is fashionable, and it immediately makes the drawing seem like *oh this is cool because it's that thing I've seen around!* When I'm just doodling and don't want to have to use my brain too much, half the time I'll draw a cat or a flower or a girl, or some basic symbol that's just an object, because I know it's going to look good, and it's going to have a certain mood. In terms of thinking of it as "real" work, I'd want it to go a little further. But a lot of people don't need it to. If your drawing is beautiful it doesn't need to go further. You can look at painters like Alex Katz, David Hockney, and Matisse, where the meaning and feeling of their work comes from their style. Certain subjects definitely become very overdone. But you can also ask, is a still life overdone? There have certainly been a ton of still lifes! With cats in illustration, it's more about style, and the context you are viewing these pieces in. You do see the same drawing of a cat a million times on Instagram. If everyone is drawing the same thing in the same style, that's when it gets exhausted, but for me it's not about content alone.

In my *work* work—something that's beyond sketchbook or doodling—I need to have a story, or a joke, or something else going on in there. A piece could essentially be a drawing of a cat, but there needs to be a reason for it. I feel the same about drawings of women. They need to be doing something or interacting in some way. There needs to be a point to it. The point can be silly, it doesn't have to be deep, but it needs to be more than just a pretty picture for me.

A lot of my projects start as self-amusement, to make myself laugh or to pass the time, which is how my book *Routine Questions for the Cat* began. In my personal relationship with my cat I like to question his behavior. I think a lot of it is pretty nonlinear, and if you examine it, it's indefensible. He's not doing anything that makes sense. If he's lying in a ridiculous pose I'll say, *Can you see yourself right now? Do you know what you look like? People are at work right now and look at you!* I like to act as if he has the capacity for self-reflection. As I was doing this regularly, sometimes the questions seemed meta. I feed him, and he continues to meow for food, and the bowl is full. I'm looking at him and I'm looking at the bowl, and I say, *Do you even know what you want?* And then I think, *Do I even know what I want?* Some of these questions, if you take them slightly outside the context of the cat are not really about the cat. Some of them feel like they're directed at me. Some of them feel like they are questions that I'm potentially asking of a young man who has wronged me in some way. It amused me to think how these questions could be applied in a wider sense. I liked the device of asking it to the cat because it made it feel more innocent. You can be way more razor sharp if it's just a dumb cat who can't answer. I try to be very deadpan, but the questions are so relentless it becomes obvious that it's about more than just the cat.

Personifying animals is a really good way of making something more relatable to a wide range of humans. If I made that same book about a twenty-seven-year-old girl living in New York fewer people would immediately relate to it. But none of us are cats, so in a weird way, we're all the cat. Personification makes the animal into an everyman. There's something hilarious about recontextualizing an animal whose thought processes and emotions are pretty simple. There's something pure about the emotions of animals, which is definitely us projecting. When a cat looks super comfy and happy it's *so* comfy and happy it's preposterous—it's the comfiest and happiest that anyone has ever been. We're always projecting a little bit. They work as stand-ins for us.

My project *Cat Encounters* began as an attempt to photodocument every cat I ever saw, and upon much soul-searching and much examination I concluded I was again using cats as a stand-in for something bigger. Initially, I was at university in Brighton and for some reason a lot of people there have outdoor cats, so I'd frequently come across one on the street. I would pet them and get to know some neighborhood ones. I wanted to start documenting them. And then I thought, *I want to document every single cat I ever see, no matter the stakes,*

no matter how bad the photograph is or if I have to photograph it in front of twenty people or run across the road, I need every single one. I was strict about it for a while, but now I don't run across the road or photograph cats when they're with other people because I started to feel like that was too invasive. I can't photograph someone in their home just because a cat is near them. I missed so many cats when I couldn't get my phone out in time. Sometimes I'm walking down the street with a friend and I have to explain that, *I'm sorry, I need to cross over for a minute*.

Regardless, this project is an exercise in completion, trying to document every one of a certain thing. It's a method of trying to control my world, and shape it, and it's a bit of an anxiety response. If I can control this thing, then I'm in control of something. If I'm documenting this aspect of my life, then my life probably isn't getting away from me. It's like journaling. Journaling makes you feel like you have a grasp on your life in some way by having a record of it.

I think I have a healthy attitude toward *Cat Encounters* now. I'm aware it's dumb and insane, but that makes me like it even more. I like that on my phone I have probably 8,000 photos—bad photos— of cats. I also enjoy walking a lot and it makes the world into a little safari. I'm always looking out for something, an adventure. It's almost a game—*I scored a point today!* It passes time and engages me with my surroundings a little more. I walk a lot and I get lost in my thoughts in a way that isn't super useful, and I find it grounding to be on the lookout. I'm not obsessing over it, I don't lose sleep over it, it doesn't occupy all of my thoughts when I'm walking, but it is something to keep me more present.

Kaye Blegvad is an illustrator and designer from London who currently lives in Brooklyn, New York. Her first illustrated book, exploring the color pink, is *The Pink Book*.

Wilson
and Winston

KELSEY MILLER

Everyone who grew up with cats has a "special cat" story in their narrative. You know, the one that makes your voice go soft when someone mentions them: *Oh, Ginger. She was a special cat.* We loved all our cats—of *course* we did, even the asshole ones who shit in the bathtub and rejected all attempted cuddles, preferring instead to spend their days sitting on the windowsill, glaring in icy judgment upon our pitiful humanity. We sobbed just as hard when those jerks died as we did over the good ones. But we're all friends here, so let's be honest: among those good ones there was one *really* good one.

It's hard to define what makes The Special Cat so special. Maybe she was exceptionally social or adventurous. Maybe he snuggled close to you when you were sick or sad, always seeming to know when you needed taking care of. It could be any number of ineffable things; I don't need to define The Special Cat for you because you know exactly who they are. You're picturing yours in your mind, right now.

Here's the thing: my Special Cat was the *most* special. Hear me out.

Wilson was born under my bed when I was five years old. It was the night of Easter Sunday and my mother was cleaning up my room while I ate tortellini in the bathtub. (She was a single mom, OK? No judgment.) I heard her yelp and, afraid that she was hurt, I jumped out of the tub and ran to my bedroom where she was staring under my bed at a *huge* litter of newborn kittens that our cat Sarah had just delivered. The number that comes to mind is thirteen, but that sounds crazy, so I'm guessing it was closer to nine or ten—which is still an absolutely bonkers number of kittens. Looking back, I have a lot of sympathy for my mother, kneeling there beside the bed wondering how the hell she was going to make it through the night with this mammoth pile of kittens *and* the wet, shrieking five-year-old running around the house shouting, "KITTENS! KITTEEEEEENS!!!!"

We lived on the top floor of a rental house owned by my mother's friends, on the densely wooded property of Sleepy Hollow

Country Club. I'm not sure if the vibe was more bucolic and secluded, like an East Coast version of the Hollywood Hills, or if it was more of a bubble of backwoods squalor on the unkempt edge of a way nicer neighborhood. Thinking about that night, though, the picture becomes pretty clear. The first thing I did was run downstairs to the basement apartment to announce the birth to the other tenants—three twentysomething guys who also served as my part-time babysitters. "WE HAD KITTENS," I screamed, then ran back upstairs, still naked with no immediate plans to get dressed and started calling the neighbors.

A few nights later, our other cat, Linda, lay down next to the television and gave birth to four more kittens. (Both she and Sarah had been impregnated by the same infamous tomcat who'd become the scourge of Tarrytown. He'd skulk around the drive-ways like Jordan Catalano, waiting for the indoor-outdoor ladies to be let out by their irresponsible owners who kept forgetting to get them spayed.) At this point, our tiny home was officially overrun with felines, and I was probably still not dressed. As soon as the kittens were big enough, my mother gathered them all up in a blanket-lined laundry basket and took them into her office in the city. She worked in the editorial department of *Gourmet* magazine, an outlet staffed almost entirely by young, single cat ladies. By the end of the day, all the kittens had been adopted. All but the one we kept for ourselves: Wilson.

Wilson had a mostly white coat with large swaths of black, like a cow. He was the kind of cat about whom people said, "He's got personality." But what Wilson really had was presence. You walked into the room and felt the need to acknowledge him, like a person: "Wilson, how've you been?" You could tell he expected this respect, and when you gave it to him, he rewarded you with his warm gaze and rich, resonant purr as he graciously received your pets. Other people often described him as regal—a benevolent King Arthur type of monarch. Now that I'm older and he is long gone, I can see what

they mean. He was never skittish, never scratched or bit or even meowed all that much. He always seemed in control of the situation, certain that one way or another, things would work out the way he wanted them to. But back then, I never thought of him like that. Because Wilson loved everyone—*but he loved me the most*.

From the beginning, Wilson was my sweetie pie. He enjoyed nothing more than to be next to me, or in my arms. I learned how to hold an animal by holding him. I think of how patient he must have been with me. Surely I squeezed too hard at first, or didn't support his hind legs. He never swatted or ran away. From the start, Wilson was as unabashedly delighted with me as I was with him. I constantly kissed the little pink bald spot beneath his left ear, and he would close his eyes, content. Sometimes I would twiddle my fingers above him and he would rise up on two legs to rub his head against them— our little game. He slept above my pillow every night, and I learned to inch myself down the bed a bit, to make space for him. If I didn't, no problem, he just slept on my head.

My mother remarried two years later and we moved into another house—one that was much busier and more bustling. My baby brother arrived shortly thereafter, and then my sister, along with a couple of other cats (both of the asshole variety, unfortunately). It was a hell of a lot of change in a short period of time, but Wilson for one adjusted to it all just fine. Each day he roamed the neighborhood, surveying the realm, receiving under-the-chin scratches from his adoring public. Most nights I stuck my head out the door before bed to call him inside, using my (very mushy but whatever) pet name for him: "Wilsy-pie, baby!" If he'd wandered far it might take a few minutes, but without fail he'd appear, his white little body trotting through the darkness toward home. Some evenings I forgot to call him or just didn't bother, knowing he was fine outside. But even on those nights he'd turn up meowing at my ground-floor bedroom window sometime before the sun came up and take his place above my pillow. My Wilsy.

A few years later, we got our first dog, Eloise, and the other cats responded in abject protest. They packed up their shit, walked over to the neighbor's house, and never came back. Wilson wasn't thrilled with our sweet, lazy black Lab, but neither was he bothered. Eloise, though utterly lovable, was dumb as a box of hair, and more interested in eating eggshells out of the compost pile than chasing a cat. Sometimes I'd notice Wilson sitting on the back steps, watching her binge on actual garbage. His expression was one of tempered disdain, not unlike the face my mother made when I put on the *Rent* CD for the nine-billionth time in a row. Sensing my gaze, Wilson would glance over his shoulder at me, and his expression would instantly shift into pure, unmitigated love. From ten feet I could hear his chainsaw purr, almost as loud as the sound of Eloise vomiting coffee grounds. Disgusting dog or not, Wilson wasn't going anywhere.

Every summer, we drove up to the Adirondacks to spend a couple weeks at my extended family's ramshackle camp. Just as my mother had done growing up, we always took our cats with us, and they enjoyed their own little summer break, prowling around the trees and sunbathing on the deck. It made me terribly nervous, taking them out of the suburbs and into true wilderness, but nothing ever happened. Losing any of them, but especially Wilson, was my deepest fear. Yet somehow, he and the others knew never to roam far, seeming to understand that they were indoor-outdoor cats whose wild instincts had gone soft thanks to their cushy lives with us humans. Their self-awareness kept them safe.

And then it happened. The summer I was thirteen, my mother, my siblings, and I drove to camp midweek. My stepfather joined us on a Friday evening after work, bringing our two current cats, Savannah and Wilson, with him. It was late when he arrived and a thunderstorm was rolling in. He scooped up the cats from the backseat and, one in each arm, headed for the house. A flash of lightning. Wilson got spooked and leaped out into the thickly wooded darkness. Gone.

We searched for him for weeks. Terrified, I spent each day

walking the property, the neighboring properties, looking under every canoe and staring up into the endless trees, desperate for a glimpse of white. I called for him, crying. I described, through sobs, his little pink bald spot to the elderly couple whose camp abutted ours. Mr. and Mrs. Abbott shook their heads, sympathetic, promising to let us know if they spotted him. "He'll turn up," everyone said, and at first I was positive he would. It was Wilson after all, the cat everybody agreed was a Special Cat. He was resourceful and smart, and always, always came home eventually. But as the summer inched toward Labor Day, no one had seen him (and we'd asked *everyone*). It became clear we would have to do the unthinkable: go home without Wilson.

I sat in the back of the car, inconsolable, all the way back to Westchester. My mother promised we would keep in touch with the neighbors, all of whom were on the lookout. The search would continue; don't give up hope. But I was a wreck. I felt like a monster, leaving without him, even if he was—*don't think it*—dead. Wilson had never once abandoned me.

The thing about loss or personal crises is that life just continues on around them. I've learned that lesson many more times as an adult. Your house gets robbed, and you go to work the next day. The doctor calls with biopsy results just as you're putting in a load of towels. And you hang up the phone and you put in the detergent, because malignant or not, you're out of towels. That fall and winter after Wilson disappeared was the first time I really understood that. I went back to school and the high drama of my adolescent life picked up right where it left off: agonizing crushes, the hell of pre-algebra, my friends and I taking turns on who got to sing the high notes when we listened to *Rent* in the back of the car. And then I would look out the window and notice the leaves had fallen, and the thought of Wilson would hit me like an ax to the heart.

Every day it got colder in Westchester, I knew it was twenty degrees colder in the Adirondacks. When snow was in the forecast,

I would check the weather upstate, too, horrified to see it had been snowing for weeks already up there. I pictured him, somehow alive but freezing and dying and wondering where I was. Why hadn't I come for him? Why had I given up? The only thing worse than thinking of his little body, wet and matted with frozen mud, was the thought that Wilson missed me. So many people think that cats don't have emotion, and it's true they don't always show it (and also true that some are simply assholes), but Wilson had shown me every day the love and happiness he felt just being near me. And so I knew with absolute certainty that if indeed he was alive, so far away, he must have been so sad.

But he probably wasn't alive. I knew that, too. Fall turned to winter. Winter dragged on into a miserable, frozen spring. We still called our upstate neighbors, but there was never any news. We called less. The truth sank in. It was a season of nonstop blizzards and gale-force winds, a brutal year even down in Westchester. He was gone. "He was a special cat," we said to one another. *He was the best cat*, I thought.

And then it happened.

Here's a nice thing about life: sometimes the life-changing calls are *good*. You're putting in a load of towels and the phone rings, and it's not the doctor but a neighbor with a cabin a few miles down the road from yours. Didn't you lose a cat last summer? Well, no promises, but someone might have seen him.

Of course, I wasn't the one washing towels and answering the phone. That was my mother, who (quite wisely) didn't tell her highly dramatic teenager every time someone reported *maybe* seeing her cat wandering around. I mean, who the hell knew if it was real? She left me to my musical theater and flailing math grades, gathering clues via telephone until she was sure. By late spring, after a handful of phone calls, she'd put the pieces together: Wilson had indeed been missing all winter. No one had seen him, and frankly, no one was really looking—especially not after the whole of the Adirondack region had been covered in icy snowbanks, four-feet deep. Then one day in April, the Abbotts opened their door to find on their deck a skinny but otherwise healthy white cat, with large black spots, and a bald spot under his left ear. He walked into their house and settled in.

When my mother finally told me, it didn't quite register. While a tiny corner of my heart was exploding with joy, the rest of me was skeptical. How? How could he possibly have survived the winter? Why hadn't we found him if he was so nearby? If it really was Wilson, why hadn't the Abbotts called us? It all seemed too good and too bizarre to be true.

At least one of these questions had an obvious answer, as we soon discovered. The Abbotts hadn't called us because Wilson—whom they called "King"—was an awesome cat! And they didn't want to give him up! Anyway, like us, they assumed he *couldn't* be our Wilson, because how on earth would our little suburban feline have survived? No, their "King" was probably a local feral cat, who was just mysteriously very good with people and comfortable living in a house for some reason. (Here I think it's worth noting that some people, like cats, are tremendous assholes.)

When I heard about the whole "King" business, I started to believe that Wilson might indeed be alive and well and living in upstate New York. Still, as my mother and I drove up to camp that May I felt a prickly dread. Even if Wilson were alive, he surely wouldn't be the same. Having lived through an Adirondack winter, he would have had to lose his soft and loving nature and turned wild, just to stay alive. What if he was too different now, and couldn't come home? What if he didn't remember me? Or worse, what if he did remember me: the girl he'd loved the most—*who had left him alone in the woods to die*.

I was a queasy, anxious mess as we knocked on the Abbotts' door. Mr. Abbott opened it and instantly, his face turned resigned.

"He's here."

Moving on autopilot, I rushed through the door, toward the back of the house and straight into the Abbotts' bedroom, where Wilson was lounging comfortably on their bed. Until I walked in. Then, his head shot up, his neck craned and eyes wide open and alert. He leaped up, ran to the edge of the bed and straight into my arms. He pressed his head against my neck hard, purring louder than my sobs. (Or so it seemed to me. To everyone else in the room, I probably sounded like a foghorn.) He was miraculously unchanged. A little skinny and his bald spot slightly weathered. But he was Wilson. He was mine. All the fear and devastation I had felt imagining his broken heart were dissolved in an instant. There was no need to wonder if he could forgive me, if he could love me still. There was no question about it.

The miracles continued when we brought Wilson home. After almost a year in the wilderness, he transitioned back to suburban life without a hitch. He was back to his old routines instantly, roaming the neighborhood, ignoring the dog, coming home each evening when I called him and settling into the spot above my pillow every night. I'd never stopped inching down the bed to make space for him.

Twenty years later, I still do it instinctively when I climb into bed next to my husband every night. We have our own cat now: Winston. I certainly didn't *mean* to give him a name that almost exactly matches Wilson's. But I'm sure there was something subconscious at play. Like all Special Cats, Wilson is woven into who I am. I don't mean that in a woo-woo way, either. In very real and tangible ways, Wilson shaped the girl I was and the woman I am. Wilson was the one who taught me how to be gentle. He taught me how to pick up on nonverbal cues, to see things like fear and contentment in a person's—or a nonperson's—body language. He taught me what loyalty looks like, what heartbreak feels like, and how abiding hope can be. He taught me that all of us, myself included, are more capable than we can possibly imagine. We can survive the unthinkable and come through with our hearts unscathed. Wilson lived almost a decade after he came home, surviving sickness and more dogs and even my departure for college. And when I came home to say goodbye, he was exactly the same. Frail as he was, he still purred like a chainsaw when he was in my arms.

Winston is different. He sleeps at the other end of the bed, curled up between our feet. He much prefers sitting in my lap to being held in my arms. He's not an asshole, thank goodness, but he's choosy in sharing his affections. "He does love you," I reassure my husband when Winston steps into my lap and snuggles in. "Yeah," he grumbles. "But he loves *you* the most."

True.

Kelsey Miller is a writer and editor based in Brooklyn, New York. She is the author of the memoir *Big Girl* and *I'll Be There for You*, a pop-culture study of the television show *Friends*.

The Cheshire Cat's Grin

Alice asked the Cheshire Cat who was sitting in a tree, "What road do I take?"
The cat asked, "Where do you want to go?"
"I don't know," answered Alice.
"Then," said the cat, "it really doesn't matter, does it?"

The Cheshire Cat is best known as a character in Lewis Carroll's 1865 book *Alice's Adventures in Wonderland*, but the expression "grinning like a cheshire cat" predates Carroll's classic by over a century and can be traced back to England's Cheshire county, a hub of dairy farms with plentiful milk and cheese. Some say cats who lived there smiled because they were so well-fed, or that the Cheshire cheese was sold in a mold that resembled a grinning cat. Carroll's Cheshire Cat is equally mysterious, with a smile as talked-about as the *Mona Lisa*'s.

Cat Lady Man

MARA ALTMAN

I have a couple of dude friends who, for lack of a better term, are cat ladies. Each of them are in their late thirties and live alone with two cats. I wanted to know how it feels to be a male cat lady in a stereotypically female-dominated role and whether or not, in their opinion, it's worth coming up with a more inclusive or specific term for men. Also, has cat-lady-dom, a lifestyle that is often wrought with misperceptions, ever presented them with challenges in their personal lives?

"If someone calls me cat lady, that's fine," said Brian Abrams, owner of and confidant to Stanley, a tabby Maine coon, and Roman, a white long hair, "but I identify more as a cat dad, even though I heard they don't actually perceive you as their dad, but as another weirder, larger cat that knows how to access the food."

I suggested "metro-cat-ual," but was aggressively turned down and made to reflect on my own out-of-touch linguistic choices. "That was a brief thing—metrosexual," Abrams said. "Of course, every man who wipes his ass or clips his nails isn't gay."

"That's not what I meant," I said, trying to set the record straight.

"And 'cat man' just sounds like a really bad comic book character," he said, pausing, "or maybe a really *good* comic book character?"

A popular Internet video called "An Engineer's Guide to Cats" describes a man with many cats as "That guy who has all those cats." Something clearly resonated because the video has over seven million views, but maybe there was a more succinct descriptor.

I threw the question over to Kevin Townley. His cats, both

American shorthair tabbies, are named Bobbi and Jones, but Jones later became Joann because his personality was revealed to be that of a worried office manager. "I think we are learning that we need a new language in general that helps us step outside these antiquated gender models," said Townley, who admits to talking to his cats, but not on too deep a level. "I'm not like, 'Should we put mom into assisted living?'" he said. "It's more like, 'How's it going? How was your day today?'"

A half hour into our conversation, he threw me a suggestion, "Maybe cat pals?"

We had our doubts the moment it left his lips.

"Look," he continued, "I wouldn't be offended if someone called me a cat lady."

It turns out that Townley actually puts the "cat lady" up on a pedestal. "She probably doesn't need a man," he explained. "She's found connection and affection with another species, like so many of us do. Maybe she has one too many or five too many cats, but it's nothing she can't handle. She's long since let go of patriarchal standards and she lives the way she wants to."

So maybe "cat lady" says it all—just like "dude" can now refer to a boy, girl, or anyone else on the gender spectrum for that matter—but I still wondered if the stereotype ever got in his way?

Townley explained that it's not his cat-lady-ness that has gotten in his way as much as the fact that he didn't train his cats properly. "I can't close the door," he said. "Well, I could, but they would literally scream at the door." Then he went on to tell me about Bobbi and Joann's morning ritual: each day at 6:15 a.m. they body slam his face from his headboard to let him know it's time to eat. "How can I bring someone into this insanity?"

Mara Altman is a San Diego–based writer. Her books include _Gross Anatomy_ and _Thanks for Coming_.

Maria Ratti

In 1949, Walter Chandoha, the husband of Maria Ratti, brought home a tiny gray kitten to their apartment in Astoria, Queens, and began taking photos of it. By the mid-1950s, he had become the go-to cat photographer in New York City and beyond, and Ratti played an important role in the process. Chandoha said of his wife, "Maria could tell by the muscular tension in the animals themselves whether they were relaxing and when I saw something of interest, I'd say 'Maria, go!' and she'd take her hands away."

On Building Home

AN INTERVIEW WITH GRACE BONNEY

My education coincided with the Internet's renaissance of art and design blogs, and as an eager student I pored over every Design*Sponge post. One of the first features I got to know and love were the home tours. They weren't merely polished interior design photos, with every-thing just so; they showed the real homes and studios of creative people. Some spaces had gallery walls made up of the artwork of friends, shelves filled with eccentric collections, and walls painted bright teal. Others were sparse and minimal, highlighting a special velvet couch or thriving houseplant. Individuality triumphed over trends. The posts were aspi-rational in a way that never made me feel inadequate. Design*Sponge fueled my excitement for the way my work and living space would grow and evolve.

Grace Bonney started Design*Sponge in 2003 when she was twenty-three years old. At the time there was no platform for the kind of handmade work she truly loved. Over the next fifteen years, Bonney grew her audience to over a million readers a month, authored two books, and launched a magazine. Though she decided to end the blog in 2019, she remains a preeminent figure promoting the value of design and female entrepreneurship.

Image after image, it's Grace Bonney's voice that stands out. Design matters to her, it makes her feel something, and she is compelled to share it. It may be as simple as a photo of a colorful bouquet of ranunculus, or her cat Turk relaxing in the upstate New York home she's renovating with her wife, Julia, but she always finds a way to tie it back to our humanity.

Bonney: I think, at our cores, we all just want to get to know each other better and find ways to connect. And one of the most intimate ways we get to do that is through people's homes. In these spaces we get to see what really matters to people and what makes them feel comfortable, safe, or inspired. We started posting home tours by just sharing one or two photos from someone's home, but as people have gotten used to living and sharing online, we now share upwards of twenty photos of people's homes. For me it's not so much about the design or trends as it is about seeing what makes someone tick and what means the most to them.

Without a doubt, people respond most strongly to interiors that have pets present. In fact, the main criticism I got when I turned in the first draft of my book was, "This book has entirely too many cats in it." To which I replied, "No such thing." Pets make us smile, they remind us to take our spaces (and the things they chew up) less seriously, and they bring any home to life. It's impossible to see a photo of a home with a happy cat or dog rolling around in the sun and not fall in love with that space and the family living inside.

I've always been a cat lady, though I think of myself now more as an animal person. I got my first cat when I was nine and my parents let me name her. I bought a naming book and everything. And the name I chose? Muffin. I should never be trusted to name anything after that decision. Thankfully all our pets after that have been rescues and came with their names, so we never changed them.

Our dogs now have taught me to open up and embrace how social pets like dogs can encourage you to be. For a decade it was just me and my cat, Turk, and we supported each other's love of naps and staying indoors. But adopting dogs has reminded me that it's good to get outside, meet new people, and brave the weather for some fresh air.

Turk is the longest and most significant relationship of my adult life. That sounds a bit much, but it's true. I adopted him one week after moving to Brooklyn by myself. I was twenty-three, knew no one in the city, and volunteered at BARC Shelter in Williamsburg, Brooklyn. Turk had been there for a year and a half with no takers— primarily because he used to be a bully. I watched him reach through the cage next to him and pull the blanket out from under another cat and I couldn't stop laughing. He was such a scrawny little punk. He has almost total body alopecia and had been burned by cigarettes as a kitten and left in a box on the street. It took him about a year to

warm up to me, but when he did, we were inseparable. He's seen me through the toughest times of my life and now that he's on his last legs at age seventeen, I'm soaking up every second I get with him.

After sixteen years of never being sick, Turk suddenly got very ill. Around Thanksgiving in 2017, he declined quickly and we found out he had both kidney and heart disease. The vet said he could have a few weeks or a few years—they didn't know how fast it would progress. We canceled our holiday travel plans and circled around him to enjoy the final weeks. But he bounced back, and even though he's started to decline again and we know the end isn't too far off, the last year with him has been an utter gift. I've showered him in love at every opportunity and I've really slowed down to pay closer attention to him. His decline paralleled a human loss we experienced at the same time, with both relationships ending in a slow, bittersweet decline. It has been such a powerful reminder to unplug and invest in real-life connections. Turk understands me like no one else and I'm so thankful for all the ways he taught me to stop, slow down, and be present for important moments.

Grace Bonney is the founder of Design*Sponge and *Good Company* magazine, and the author of *Design*Sponge at Home* and *In the Company of Women*. She lives in Upstate New York with her wife.

The
Anniversary Cat

NOËL WELLS

I always wanted a cat. I grew up with approximately eight different cats in my family's home. From Winston to CeeCee to Dixie to Portia to Milo, I loved them very much, but I was always certain that none of them were "my cat." Of our felines, George was definitely my stepdad's cat—a fluffy, overfed, and obstinate Maine coon. Playful when he wanted to be, he ruled the roost like a lazy king, and though he was fun for short periods of time, like his human counterpart, he was known to attack without warning. Dixie, a thin, skittish tortoiseshell, was definitely my mom's cat. I wanted desperately to love her, though she would clench up any time I went near her, putting up with my affection for a few seconds before wriggling away and leaving a few scratches behind, mirroring all too accurately the human mother/daughter dynamic in the house. Surrounded by so many cats, I didn't understand why none of the cats seemed to "click" with me, and in many ways, this made me feel unlovable. Even having no cat was a perfect reflection of my internal strife, a seeming loner among many.

How cats and people find each other could be a matter of symbiotic convenience, though over time I have come to believe it takes a dash of luck, and perhaps even a matter of cosmic timing. The first time I was on the receiving end of fate, I was seventeen. Like any classic case of true love I wasn't looking for her. Arriving home from high school, there she was. A cat, all white with a little brown splotch on her face, sitting on our carport. She and I locked eyes. I greeted her warmly, hoping to coax her down for a little pet. And to my surprise, not only did she come, she came bounding toward me, showering me with rubs. She was a pretty, delicate Manx cat, seemingly fancy and pedigreed, so I assumed she belonged to someone else, and I went inside. The next day, however, she was there again, peering over the carport, meowing down at me. So ravenous was she for my affection, I decided to open the front door of my house and invite her in. Without hesitation she slipped inside, and from there on out I had a cat. I named her Cynthia. She slept in my bed every night.

She let me pick her up, she let me kiss her stomach and play with her paws. She snuggled with me, watched TV with me, drooled on me. I taught her to play fetch. She would even go on walks with me. People would comment on how friendly she was for a cat, but despite her gregarious and outgoing nature, she had one person she loved the most, and it was me. Sometimes I wondered, "Why me? Why does this awesome cat love me?" And I would tell myself that she was fond of me because I was the first to feed her. To me it felt like I had hit the lottery, and I had just better accept my good fortune. She and I remained loving friends until I went to college and I left her at my parents' home.

In college, I found what I thought was my human soul mate, a boyfriend I so quickly attached to that we found ourselves moving in together as soon as we could. Knowing how much I missed Cynthia, for our one-year anniversary he got me a gift, a teenage bruiser of a kitten that I would name Mr. Feeny. At the time, he said the choice for this particular kitten was made merely on the grounds that this was the one who had clung to him, desperate to get away from the other kittens and begin life with humans. So the boyfriend, not having any other idea of how to choose a kitten, took him home. Me, still not sensitive to the way fate would play its hand, thought that was as good of a reason as any, and subscribing to the nurture version of nature versus nurture, I was excited to imprint a dynamic similar to the one I had with Cynthia. But try as I might, Mr. Feeny's personality was firmly resistant to my influence. While Cynthia was delicate, needy, and sweet, Mr. Feeny was a rabble-rouser, playful, rambunctious, energetic, and slightly devilish. I quickly accepted how different they were from each other, although he did have several things in common with her. He was incredibly friendly. He slept with me every night. He let me pick him up, kiss his stomach, play with his paws. I taught him to play fetch. By the time we moved into the studio-like top story of a Victorian, I would leave the window open for him to come and go as he pleased, and he would excitedly peek his head over the roof when I came home from school, and go on walks with me around the block. And just like Cynthia, Mr. Feeny was certainly, unequivocally, my cat.

=^-^=

I'm not sure exactly when my relationship with my boyfriend began to take a turn. Looking back now I can see it was brought on by his struggles with his grades and an addiction to Adderall which he had easily acquired from a random school doctor. Though the personality shift was dramatic, it slipped in through the back door, and went straight for my cat. "You love your cat more than me" became a favorite refrain, and soon I went from being bemused by the accusation to being constantly on the defensive. When the fights started to escalate, I would plead with him, saying, "You're upsetting Mr. Feeny!" To which he would spit, "You're anthropomorphizing him. Cats don't feel. Cats don't have emotions." I found it strange that he made an enemy out of a cat, but subconsciously, I must have known that by attacking him, he was also implying that MY emotions weren't real, and it was only a matter of time before he would say as such, and any pleas I made to get through to him began to be met with increasing venom, and soon, punishing silence. As the emotional abuse spun further and further out of control, and I became more isolated from my friends and from the outside world, I would find the only place I could feel safe would be the hallway closet, where I would sit and hide in the dark. Mr. Feeny, the supposed cat without feelings, would come into the dark with me and silently sit by my side as I cried.

Mr. Feeny and I eventually moved out, and it seemed like life returned to normal, though I wouldn't know until years later how savagely the human relationship had destroyed my self-esteem, allowing the self-loathing that had haunted me since childhood to take a darker hold. I continued school, moved in with a new, kind

boyfriend. Mr. Feeny was still Mr. Feeny, though now he seemed to reflect some of my new neuroses. He seemed more skittish and became afraid of strangers. Like me, he would only let humans he trusted near him. But those he did let near him were always impressed by how friendly he was. He continued sleeping with me and loving me, his loyalty never waning, though sometimes I felt, deep down inside, that I didn't deserve his love . . . and over the years I wondered why someone like me deserved something as loyal as him. Yet despite my doubts, he gently persisted in staying by my side. We went through other human relationships and moves. He lived in shitty apartments with me and then fancy apartments in the Hollywood Hills. Years passed. People would ask me how I got him, and I would say, "Oh, he was given to me randomly for an anniversary."

I started going to therapy, and as I worked through my anxieties, I slowly regained my self-worth. I began to not only unpack what had happened to me in college, but also started noticing that as I seemed to come out of my shell, so did Mr. Feeny. Each step I took in recovering self-confidence, he seemed to mirror. Suddenly, he wasn't so skittish around strangers. Suddenly, he was strutting around like he did when he was a kitten. And as I started to learn to accept myself, I began to realize that my cat loved me, not because I just fed him or because he imprinted on me as a kitten, but because we shared some window of love, and he loved me because I loved him. The love my cat had for me, and the loyalty he reflected, was somehow a peek into my own capacity for the same. That perhaps, maybe, just maybe, my cat was more than just a cat. That maybe he was my cat because this was always meant to be, that he and I were assigned to each other in this lifetime to be companions in this cosmic window of experience. Our mission was to grow up together and reveal a little of our souls to each other. He was always meant to be "my cat." And I always wonder, if everyone says he's such a friendly cat, what does that mean about me?

Noël Wells is an actor, comedian, musician, and writer. She wrote, directed, and starred in the film *Mr. Roosevelt* and released her debut album in spring 2019.

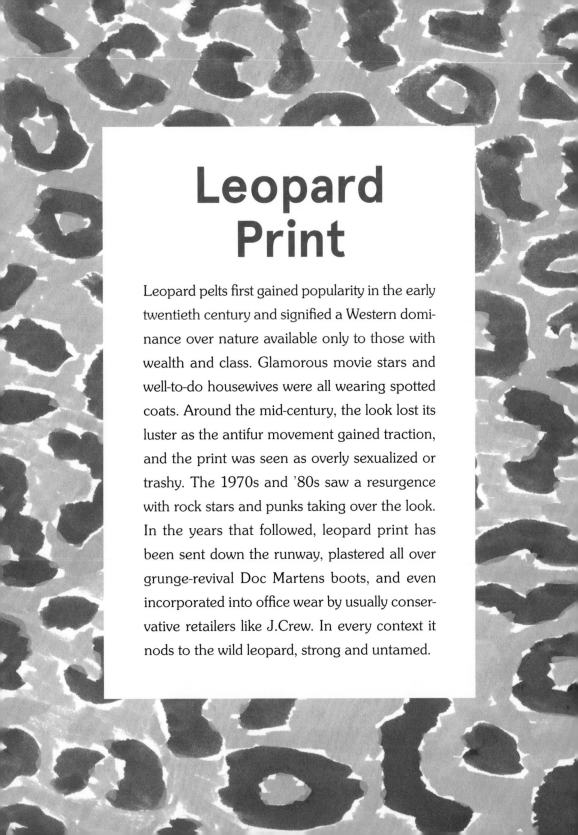

Leopard Print

Leopard pelts first gained popularity in the early twentieth century and signified a Western dominance over nature available only to those with wealth and class. Glamorous movie stars and well-to-do housewives were all wearing spotted coats. Around the mid-century, the look lost its luster as the antifur movement gained traction, and the print was seen as overly sexualized or trashy. The 1970s and '80s saw a resurgence with rock stars and punks taking over the look. In the years that followed, leopard print has been sent down the runway, plastered all over grunge-revival Doc Martens boots, and even incorporated into office wear by usually conservative retailers like J.Crew. In every context it nods to the wild leopard, strong and untamed.

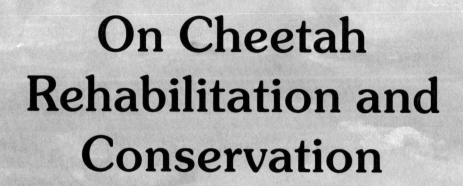

On Cheetah Rehabilitation and Conservation

AN INTERVIEW WITH LISA KYTÖSAHO

Lisa Kytösaho nuzzles a full-grown cheetah, her long brown hair windswept. She lies in the sand, another cheetah sprawled comfortably over her arm like an oversize house cat. She scratches him under the chin and he purrs loudly, turning to rest his head on her chest. It looks like she's living in a dream, running through the South African savanna with strong spotted cats by her side. But Kytösaho is a professional, careful to let anyone following along on Instagram know that wildlife are not pets. "Wildlife belong in the wild," she writes. "I work hands-on with them as rescues to rehabilitate and teach them to hunt so they can go back to a natural habitat."

Originally from Sweden, Kytösaho is the head of Western Cape Cheetah Conservation (WCCC) in Cape Town, South Africa. At twenty-seven, she's already been working with cheetahs for ten years. Kytösaho completed her education in animal care focusing on wildlife, and from there moved to Namibia for an internship. In Namibia she learned to rehabilitate wildlife, release cheetahs, and monitor them after release, as well as set up wildlife release sites. When she had the opportunity to take a paid position in South Africa with Cape Cheetah, she immediately accepted. I wrote to Kytösaho to learn more about her work and the animals she cares for.

Kytösaho: Cheetahs are solitary animals in the wild, which means they live alone most of the time and hunt alone. They are big cats built for speed and their whole body is adapted and perfected for running. Cheetahs have an amazingly light body structure and a small head, nonretractable claws for gripping the ground when running, a very flexible spine, and a tail as a rudder for balance. Their natural habitat is savanna, shrubland, desert, and grassland as they need vast spaces to do their sprints for hunts. They have incredible eyesight and can spot prey up to three miles (five km) away, which I find fascinating. Once they've spotted their target far away, they will silently stalk their way closer until they can pick up a chase. Cheetahs are endangered, with the conservation status "Vulnerable." There are just over 6,500 mature individuals in the world.

Cape Cheetah was founded by Damien Vergnaud. He saved the first cheetahs and started the program and mission to help captive-born cheetahs live a natural life again. We rescue ill-treated captive individuals throughout South Africa, rehabilitate them, and relocate out into natural areas. The cheetahs come from all different backgrounds: some were abused, some have severe medical conditions, and some were previously kept as exotic pets. We also work toward having healthy populations of wild and semi-wild cheetahs and relocating them into protected areas. Additionally, we have a sanctuary for the individuals who cannot be completely rehabilitated. Currently we are expanding and working on bigger release sites and possibilities for translocation of wildlife to larger areas in Africa, as well as becoming involved in protecting the wild populations.

There is absolutely more to this job than cuddling with the animals. In fact, that is the highlight of my job, and is rarer than you might think due to all the other tasks. The majority of the work includes removing excrement, raking, carrying heavy water buckets and straw bales, repairing fencing, and so much more. A day typically starts at seven in the morning prepping the cheetahs' meals. I spend about thirty minutes portioning and preparing the food depending on what it is they are being fed that day—it's always different. The main food prep is normally done in advance, so the morning is mostly dividing up the portions. Then I go to the cheetahs that are in the first rehab stage. I clean all their camps in a very specific routine I've created to ensure top hygiene. I also walk around the areas and look for any snakes or scorpions, and I clean out the indoor area they have free access to in case of cold weather or rain. When all areas are clean, the cheetahs are fed, and once they are finished eating the area is cleaned again.

After this, I drive to the reserve. Here I monitor the wild cheetahs, look over health, and do any upkeep on their space: checking fence lines, water troughs, and water holes within the reserve. After,

I go to the wild rehab area where we have individuals in a dehuman-ization process. This means they are becoming less used to human interaction and reintroduced to wild behaviors. These cheetahs are fed in the morning so I bring their food and feed it to them. They are considered semi-wild and in rehabilitation, so they live in large areas that are managed differently than where the Stage 1 cheetahs live.

I do have some other animals I tend to after this, but this concludes the majority of the morning routine. Then it is time for training. I bring out the Stage 1 rehabilitation cheetahs and do exer-cise runs. They are transported to free open areas and we have a lure that is dragged on the ground with a specially modified machine. They love this exercise and it keeps them fit, healthy, and strong. They get free rein to do what they feel like after they are finished with the runs.

This continues until the early afternoon. My schedule is never fixed because it depends on the cheetahs, but at some point I have lunch. In the summer it's extremely hot, so we take a break during the hottest part of the day. We start up again when it cools down and take time for some hunting and exploring. Whether it becomes a hunt or not is completely according to the natural elements—noth-ing is set up or staged. We let the cheetahs roam open spaces with no fences and they can pick up a chase and try to hunt. While they're in the natural space, they're able to learn many valuable lessons and necessary skills, even simply how to walk within that space. I support the cheetahs in certain aspects of the hunts and can guide and help them when they need it.

When this activity is finished we get ready for the evening cheetah run with the semi-wild cheetahs. This is within the cheetah reserve and is viewed by the safari guests from the top of a tower, so there's some pressure to have it ready at the perfect time. When the semi-wild cheetahs have completed their run, they are fed and then the safari guests are given an educational speech. The sun will have set by this time, and the work is almost done. I make one last tour of

cheetahs for the night. I prepare the inside sleeping areas with a nice warm straw, check their water supply, and make sure no snakes or scorpions are in their areas.

This concludes a normal day without any specific extra work or tasks. Many days, I also work on an individual basis rehabilitating cheetahs who are in all different stages. This all depends on the need—I may be getting them ready for a move, providing maintenance, or any other special projects.

Instagram has brought a large, positive impact as it has enabled me to speak with a louder voice for the animals and this cause. I believe it will only improve in the future, showing people how they can get involved and help us in this work for cheetahs! Instagram encourages me to share what I'm doing and combines my love for this work and photography. It is a great platform for this.

While I receive the occasional negative comment from someone who doesn't understand what I'm doing, I don't let it cloud my mind too much. There are some misconceptions that these cheetahs are my pets, but I work hard to make sure it doesn't get interpreted as such. I try to showcase many of the activities that are a part of the rehabilitation program. Regardless, some people still just see it the way they want to without doing further research or even reading the captions to the images. I don't like that part, but I do still believe that through my presence online and with this platform I have a great opportunity to speak for the animals and have more impact than if I were not doing it at all. I try to see social media as a positive addition rather than a need or obligation. My first priority is focusing on my work and my life. Each animal deserves their freedom, and we are the bridge to giving it back to them.

Lisa Kytösaho is from Sweden and now lives in South Africa, where she's the head of Western Cape Cheetah Conservation.

Cats in Nineteenth-Century Japanese Art

Woodblock prints became popular during Japan's Edo period (1603–1868), as the images could be mass produced and sold cheaply. People were looking for fun and fashionable art, and this included all sorts of popular subjects, especially cats. Many of these images are purely decorative and often funny. There are cats doing regular cat things and cats with people, and then there are cats dressed up as people doing everything from dancing, to getting dressed, to riding in horse-drawn carriages.

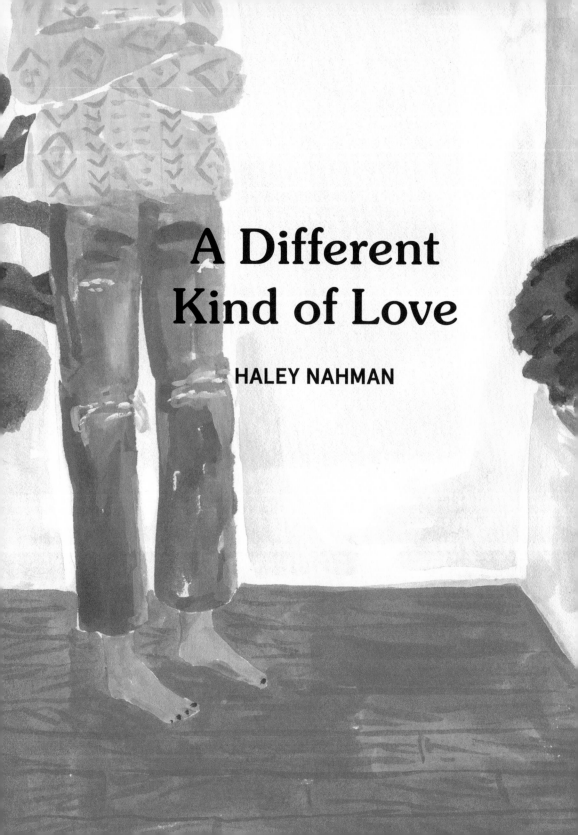

A Different Kind of Love

HALEY NAHMAN

My cat's face is so flat he can place it flush against a wall. He does this from time to time, I assume as a means of escape from his captive life, the way I might bang my head against a door if I were enclosed in a small space, never permitted to venture out.

Bug is an indoor cat. Not by choice, but due to that fact that his survival skills start and end with standing over his food bowl for entire afternoons, eating at a speed of two granules per minute. Sometimes when I'm walking in Brooklyn (I'm an outdoor cat), I imagine seeing Bug emerge from between two parked cars, like one of the many strays I've spotted on Starr Street. I imagine Bug, with his fluffy gray-and-white mane, impossibly small pink nose, head round like a plate, fighting street cats for his cut of a leftover deli sandwich and then searching for a tilted, elevated nonslip bowl to eat it off of, like the one he has at home by a brand called Pawmosa.

He could never hack it out there, and so he sits on the windowsill and looks outside or chases a feather on a string like it's a real bird, or chips away at his long-term goal of napping on every square foot of my apartment. He is always there when I return: after long days of work, after trips thousands of miles away, after wandering around New York until my feet hurt. No matter where I am—laughing, crying, drinking—he is home—sleeping, licking, nibbling, in the same five-hundred-square-foot space.

His life may sound pathetic, but his unbridled confidence and disinterest in my affections say otherwise. He doesn't care for my sappy overtures and incessant questioning (How was your day? How are you feeling? What are you thinking about?) and would much prefer to sit three to five feet away from me or out of my sight completely. Sometimes I tell him I love him and he falls asleep. Sometimes he lets me scratch his belly while he looks across the room, dead-eyed, like he's doing me a favor.

I hold Bug captive for his own good. His predecessor, an orange-and-white hamster I fell in love with at Petco, was less lucky. Judi Dench spent 80 percent of her life trying to escape her habitat,

sometimes gnawing on the bars for hours at a time. I used to say the worst day of her life was the day I brought her home and locked her in her cage—but then I didn't yet know that unlocking it would be the end of her. One day, out of guilt, I finally let her run free in my apartment. For months after that she enjoyed an hour outside of her cage every day, roaming a world full of spaces she could squeeze through, but shouldn't, and heights she wanted to scale, but couldn't. I won't finish this story except to say I loved her so much I set her a little too free. Judi taught me that loving someone doesn't always mean giving her what she wants.

But before I got Bug, before I got Judi, I was a dog person. When I lived in San Francisco, I was a professional dog sitter, sometimes taking in multiple dogs at a time. There was Walker, the shih tzu who quietly napped on me all day. Roux, the spaniel who loved running around with my socks. There was Jumbo the Chihuahua, Giblet the bichon frise, Doogie and Simon the poodles, Freeman the Pomeranian, Jax the wheaten terrier. One time I saw Jax on the train during my commute home, months after I'd babysat him, and we looked at each other the whole ride like stifled, long-lost lovers. It was that kind of mutual affection I cherished about dogs—and still do. I love how they love me unconditionally, every day, at any hour. It's an easy kind of devotion. An ideal one for a sap like me.

Cats, on the other hand, preach a different kind of love. When I fill up Bug's food bowl, he is not excited. When I pick him up, he clamors to be put down. His tail does not wag when I enter a room nor has he ever licked my face. He does not shake. He does not sit. He does not fetch. There is little proof, in fact, that he's ever been happy to see me, but I go on loving him anyway. My love for him is pure in that way, I think, because it asks for nothing in return beyond the pleasure of caring for him. Of cleaning out his eyes every morning. Or cutting poop out of the fur around his butt when the situation calls for it. Or being woken up in the middle of the night by his nearby kneading. And every once in a while, between the brush-offs, he curls up behind my computer as I work, or sits next to me on the couch with little fanfare, or follows me around the house absent-mindedly, and I'm reminded our affection is mutual if I'm patient.

I have a lot to learn from how he moves through his little captive world. Because despite all evidence to the contrary, Bug doesn't think he needs me, and in that sense, he's free to love me as he pleases.

Haley Nahman is a Brooklyn, New York–based writer and the deputy editor at Man Repeller.

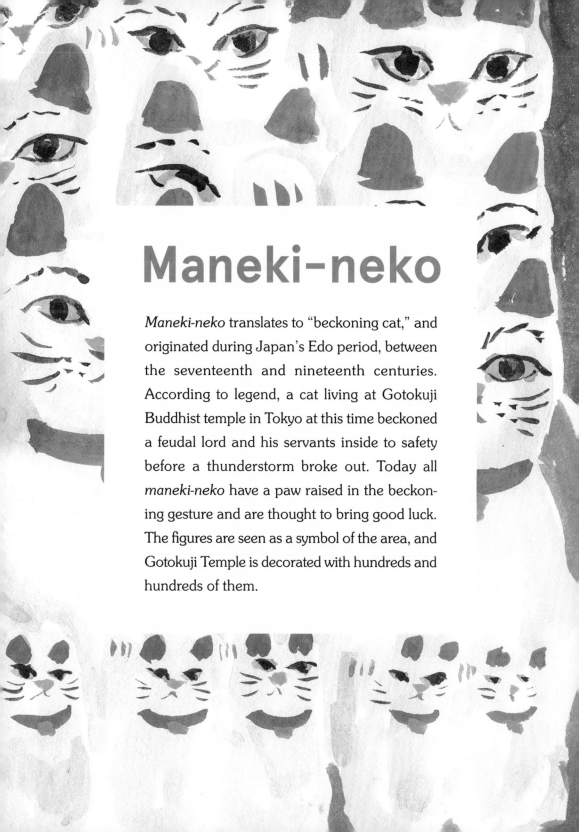

Maneki-neko

Maneki-neko translates to "beckoning cat," and originated during Japan's Edo period, between the seventeenth and nineteenth centuries. According to legend, a cat living at Gotokuji Buddhist temple in Tokyo at this time beckoned a feudal lord and his servants inside to safety before a thunderstorm broke out. Today all *maneki-neko* have a paw raised in the beckoning gesture and are thought to bring good luck. The figures are seen as a symbol of the area, and Gotokuji Temple is decorated with hundreds and hundreds of them.

On Pedigreed Cats and Shows

AN INTERVIEW WITH ALLENE TARTAGLIA

The documentary *Catwalk: Tales from the Cat Show Circuit*, which I streamed on Netflix in bed with my purebred yet thoroughly unsophisticated cats, follows several exhibitors as they hop from show to show, letting us in on their motivations and wildest dreams to win it all. One standout scene shows a gray-haired judge examining a marmalade pouf of a Persian. "I have goosebumps," he states calmly, looking up. "thirty-two years of judging, this is one of the finest cats I've ever judged." It is funny, his somber sincerity coupled with what is assumed to be the inherent frivolity of a cat show. But the shows must have a purpose, too, beyond a mere "beauty contest" as one exhibitor sums it up. Right?

The Cat Fanciers' Association (CFA) is the world's largest registry of pedigreed cats. It was founded in 1906 as a nonprofit and licensed its first cat shows that same year. CFA is now headquartered in Alliance, Ohio. Along with its offices, the CFA building in Alliance houses the Feline Historical Museum and its collection of fine art, artifacts, historical documents, cat show memorabilia, and a library of over two thousand books about cats. CFA's website lists such notable acquisitions as an early 1900s wooden cat carrier, the silver collar awarded to the winner of the first Madison Square Garden cat show in New York City in 1895, and a cat house designed by Frank Lloyd Wright. I hope to visit one day.

Allene Tartaglia is the executive director of CFA. I reached out to ask her a little more about the organization and what, exactly, these cat shows are all about.

Tartaglia: I grew up with dogs—large dogs such as the golden retriever and German shepherd. It wasn't until I was in my late thirties that I got my first cat and I was hooked. I realized that cats are just as affectionate as dogs but in a different way. Cats are better cuddlers than dogs and are much easier to take care of. Interestingly, cats are considered more a women's pet and men shy away from having a cat because they think cats are feminine. I have found that men who love and appreciate cats are "real" men who are confident enough in themselves to love a cat and not be concerned about what other people think.

My first cat was a Devon rex and I adore the breed. I love their cute, pixie faces, the big ears, their curly coats, and the wonderful personality. The most recent breed I've fallen in love with, though, is the Cornish rex. They are like little people and are fascinated by everything. Their ears are even larger than the Devons and the marcelled coat is so soft. They tend to be a little smaller than the Devons and maintaining their svelte form is easy because they are so active. Currently, I have one Devon and two Cornish pets. I don't breed or show but I sure am glad there are people who do so I can continue having these wonderful treasures in my life.

I've worked for CFA in one capacity or another since 1982. Currently, I am the executive director and I am responsible for interacting with the board as well as running the office. A little bit of everything, pretty much. Although our mission has remained essentially the same, today we are more focused on the welfare and inclusion of *all* cats, pedigreed or not.

I am involved with the organization of the one show that CFA itself produces, the CFA International Cat Show. It is the largest and most prestigious show that CFA has. A typical show has three parts: the judging area where the cats are brought to be handled and judged, the benching area where cats wait to be called to a ring, and the vendor area, a space where various cat-related products are showcased and available for sale, such as cat trees, grooming supplies, cat food, and more. The judging area normally consists of six or more individual "rings" either around the perimeter of the show hall or in the middle. The benching area consists of tables and cages for the cats where exhibitors set up with decorations and settle in for the one or two days of the show. It should be noted that cats are *never* left in a show hall overnight. The owners always take their cats with them at the end of the day. The benching area is located for convenience to the judging rings since there is a lot of

back-and-forth traffic to and from the judging and benching area as people take their cats to the judging rings to be judged. The vendor area is typically located toward the front of the show hall near the entrance.

There are many reasons for a cat show. A cat show offers the opportunity for a breeder to have their cat or cats seen by a trained judge, which will help them know if their breeding program is on the right track. It's important to have the opinion of others since we all tend to be a little "blind" when we are emotionally involved. A cat is judged on how well he or she meets the show standard, conformation, as well as temperament. Conformation is important for a breeding program and temperament is important even beyond the show ring and cattery. Anyone looking for a pedigreed pet wants not only the predictable look and traits but they also want a well-socialized cat with a good temperament.

Companion cats, also known as household pets, can be shown at CFA shows and CFA also offers a showing category for pedigreed cats that have been neutered or spayed, called the premiership class.

A cat show provides a great social atmosphere for cat exhibitors to share challenges, successes, and in general, have a great time. Someone looking to add a pedigreed pet to their home will be able to interact with the various breeds and meet a breeder in person. Some shows have an agility course for cats and it's always fun to watch. Some cats whiz through the course, some not so much. Many shows invite local shelters to bring cats and kittens available for adoption and this is a very popular attraction. CFA participants give back to the community whenever possible.

The preservation of pedigreed cats will ensure we don't lose these wonderful breeds and their predictable temperament and traits. Pedigreed cats are usually more social than non-pedigreed cats because they are handled by humans on a daily basis since birth. Few people realize that pedigreed cats are 3 percent or less of the general cat population. Responsible breeders have a six-month or more waiting list for kittens. Breeders promote neuter/spay, keeping cats indoors, not declawing, and are available to answer any questions a new pet owner might have. They practice good feline husbandry and are careful to not perpetuate undesirable traits. A breeder wants you to have a healthy and loving kitten as much as you do.

Allene Tartaglia is the executive director of the Cat Fanciers' Association.

Cat-Eye Glasses

Inspired by harlequin masks, Altina Schinasi designed the first pair of cat-eye glasses in the late 1930s. Aiming to rebuke the old adage that "boys don't make passes at girls who wear glasses," Schinasi designed this new pair of frames to flatter the face. Her first prototypes were cut out of paper. Audrey Hepburn is credited with popularizing the sunglass version in 1961's *Breakfast at Tiffany's*.

Roscoe

ASHLEY REESE

I was never supposed to be a cat person.

In fact, I was never supposed to be a pet person in general. Aside from an ill-fated carnival goldfish, I never had pets growing up and, to this day, sometimes find their presence in homes a bit strange—the select set of animals we humans happily allow free rein in our homes, leaving an endless trail of hair in their wake. It's sort of weird when you really think about it. But while I always held a soft spot for dogs, I never cared much for cats.

I found the aloofness of cats frustrating and their temperaments too unpredictable for comfort. They were cold compared to dogs, who seemed to have an unlimited supply of affection and loyalty that I assumed a cat could never possess. Cats were a presence I tolerated at friends' homes and enjoyed at a safe distance in the form of cute viral videos.

And then I met Roscoe.

The first time I saw Roscoe he was popping out of my then-roommate's coworker's tote bag. He was around three years old and oddly calm during the unplanned visit. It didn't take long for him to get comfortable exploring our Crown Heights, Brooklyn apartment. His light orange fur contrasted against the bright turquoise walls of my bedroom, and his olive eyes peered around the space with complete serenity. I was no cat expert by any means, but I knew that cats tended to freak out in new environments. Roscoe didn't, and happily perched himself on the windowsills or stretched out on the hardwood floor, completely relaxed.

But his stay was brief, lasting only a couple of hours while my roommate and Roscoe's owner chatted. Meanwhile, Roscoe made an impression on me that I couldn't shake off, and luckily didn't have to. Almost a year later Roscoe's owner needed a place to keep him for a week or so while she moved into a new apartment, and my roommate and I agreed to watch him.

A couple of weeks turned into nearly two months. My roommate wasn't nearly as taken with this cat who, for all his cuteness, was a little needy and a little devious. He had a tendency to poke his head into our water glasses, paw at our dinner plates, and yowl relentlessly if he was locked out of our bedrooms at night. In fact, Roscoe's need to have free rein of our bedrooms got so bad that I had to barricade my door from time to time to get an ounce of privacy. But that didn't stop Roscoe from pressing his head against my door, his strong cranium easily pushing my increasingly heavy blockades. (And after all that persistence, he'd sniff around, crawl onto my bed for a few minutes, then glibly prance out of the room.)

"His eyes weird me out," my roommate said one day, her honeymoon period with Roscoe long over. "They look like snake eyes in the morning." But for all of the frustrations he racked up during his two-month stay—stinking up his litter box, barfing on my bed one time, keeping me up at night—I grew fond of him. I looked forward to his eager meows when I entered my apartment, I loved seeing him sleep at the end of my bed on a Sunday afternoon, and I didn't mind him nestling onto my chest when I was busy working on my laptop, boldly asserting himself as a far more important entity than my browser.

And then, he was gone, reunited with his owner. My roommate was relieved, and while I was happy not to deal with a stinky litter box every morning, I missed the big orange lug.

I eventually accepted that I'd likely never see Roscoe again, but several months later my luck changed: Roscoe's owner was giving him away. She said taking care of Roscoe and her older dog was too much work. Between Roscoe and the dog, her choice was easy, leaving Roscoe's fate unclear. At the time, my boyfriend and I had recently moved into our own place, but our landlord had a firm no pet policy. So when Roscoe's owner, knowing my affection for him, asked if I wanted to take him, I was heartbroken that there was no way we could get Roscoe to stay with us.

But I had an idea.

My boyfriend's family lived in rural Western New York, where they owned several cats. It was a cat haven—acres of roaming grass-land with little concern for predators or cars during the day, and an old farmhouse with lots of cozy corners to lurk about at night. Before I knew it, I was buying a cat carrier and my boyfriend was filling out a car rental application.

We picked up Roscoe in the morning, mixing half a Benadryl capsule into some lox-flavored cream cheese we fed to him before whisking him away. His days of being a Brooklyn cat were over. Little did he know he was pivoting to country cat. Aside from the occa-sional curious meow from the backseat during our six-hour drive, he didn't complain. And when he arrived at my boyfriend's parents' home—secluded from the other cats at first—he seemed fine. I thought he would transition easily, just as he did when he had stayed with me the year prior.

I thought wrong!

Part of me knows I should have seen it coming. I'm an only child; I can't imagine waking up one day and having to share a space with others. But my prospects for Roscoe were overly optimis-tic. Roscoe might have lived with a dog for most of his life, but he certainly hadn't lived with other cats. Going from being the only cat in a small Brooklyn apartment to one of six cats in a big ol' house was a huge adjustment. He hissed at the other cats and used his size to assert power over his new brothers and sisters who had been there long before him. I was afraid that I had made a huge mistake, that my selfish desire to have easy access to Roscoe wasn't worth him being in a stressful environment. After a week, my boyfriend and I went back to Brooklyn and I was left feeling slightly disappointed, but also hopeful the adjustment period would get easier.

That was in 2016.

Three years later, Roscoe is bigger and more beautiful than ever, absolutely spoiled rotten by my boyfriend's family with treats and endless praise and cuddles. He's still terrified to go outside, but every time I come for a visit, he seems pleased, tail lolling happily as he reclines on the dining table, body lazily draped over the edge of the kitchen sink like a leopard on a tree branch. And he's still as vocal as ever at the prospect of getting a nibble of human food (he loves pastrami), and as proud as ever to share the results of his hunting skills with his humans (he hunts socks and meows unceasingly about them in the middle of the night).

But in many ways, he's different. Maybe it's age, but he's more sensitive, easier to anger than when he stayed with me years earlier. There are still a couple of cats that he doesn't get along with, and he makes his displeasure clear whenever they get too close. I sometimes feel a pang of regret when I wonder if Roscoe was meant to live in a cat-free home, despite how much care and attention he receives on a daily basis. Are some cats naturally moody? Am I reading too much into petty interactions between animals? Am I just not seeing the full picture? Should I call the guy from *My Cat from Hell*?

But then I feel my little guest bed sink slightly in the middle of the night. Without turning on a light I know it's Roscoe, eager for company, warmth, and solace in the quiet of the night, purring as I gently scratch behind his ears. He might be a bit of a drama queen, and he's certainly more rotund than he used to be, but at his core he's the same cat—the *first* cat—that I fell in love with all those years ago. And despite the fact that I only see him a few times a year, I feel like Roscoe's surrogate mother, like he's as much mine as the family he sees every day.

Roscoe turned me into a cat person, and for that I'll always thank him . . . with pastrami.

≋ ♥ ≋

Ashley Reese is a writer from Los Angeles living in New York. She is a staff writer at Jezebel.

On Cats and Home

AN INTERVIEW WITH AMINA KIM

In the summer of 2018 I packed up my comfortable one-bedroom apartment in Brooklyn, New York and ordered two TSA-approved cat carriers in preparation to fly into the unknown. I had just done something that on paper sounded reckless: purchased an old tennis club in the middle of California's Anza-Borrego Desert State Park with Adil, my boyfriend of 18 months. It cost considerably less than buying an apartment in New York, and plus, we were going to build Shangri-la. There was a lot to be anxious about, but I was mostly worried about the cats.

At JFK, because we had animals, we were ushered into our own line to quickly pass through security. But first, we had to remove Aaron and Lacy from their carriers and hand-carry them through the body scanner. This was the part I had been preparing for, just shy of rolling out a map of the airport and plotting our route in red ink. Adil would first carry Lacy—who loathed being held—and then I would take Aaron. When it was my turn, I took a deep breath and laced my fingers firmly around the harness I had wrestled onto his tiny chest for this moment.

I stepped through the archway as Adil was zipping Lacy back into her case and turned to the conveyor belt for the other one, but it was nowhere in sight. It was still on the other side, caught behind other baggage that had snuck ahead. My worst nightmare was losing my grip and Aaron darting off into the depths of the airport. All I could do as Aaron writhed in my arms, claws out, was meditate on a phrase from a YouTube video we had watched where a vet demonstrates how to hold a cat: "Squish. That. Cat!"

We made it to California. The pills the vet had given me didn't really work—both cats woke up on the plane, and Lacy peed all over herself. But we made it. My mom picked us up at the San Diego airport and drove us three hours into the desert. Both cats came into the front seat and curled up on my lap. Lacy's pee-soaked fur seeped through the thin fabric of my black leggings and I didn't care.

It's easy to say that the desert gets quite hot in the summer, but it's another thing entirely to step out of an air-conditioned Kia onto a 118-degree driveway at dusk. I had opened the oven to check on dinner, and then crawled inside. We quickly deposited the cats in their new home, belonging to Adil's parents, Amina and Christian. The house was one in a Palm Desert gated retirement community boasting almost five thousand houses built in a vague Spanish style and surrounded by native desert landscaping. Inside it was airy, partially carpeted, and very quiet. The cats loved it.

Our property was an hour's drive away. We had an office, a clubhouse with a full kitchen, four tennis courts, a pool, and over two acres of unused land where we parked a tiny camper trailer to sleep in. But we didn't have a house, at least until we could build ourselves one. "It's an alternative lifestyle," I liked to say, with a laugh. I had initially thought we might fix up the clubhouse for the cats to live in, and during the day they'd be free to roam around the gated grounds, but it soon became clear I didn't want to put them through that. This was going to be a business, and guests would be in and out of the clubhouse. A gate could be left open, and the area was rife with coyotes. We saw them casing the perimeter of our land and loitering in the front yard of the elementary school. I couldn't help but find them adorable, as long as they preyed on the native rabbits and quail, not my cats. Aaron and Lacy would stay safe in Palm Desert with their new mom, Amina Kim.

Kim: From my experience in Morocco, people like cats and see them as special and cute—sacred even—but they don't care about dogs. They will feed and talk to a stray cat but ignore or chase off a dog. In homes, cats are treated like part of the family. They are fed people's food—not specialty cat food. But like other family members, they are seen as relatively self-sufficient. They can take care of themselves and come and go as they please. Cats are given their own sleeping area, and are not allowed on furniture, seating, and especially not in beds. In our culture, the pet does not go on the bed! It was a shock coming to the United States, where pets are really babied, even pushed around in strollers.

In Morocco there are residential streets in front of homes or in markets, and on the streets, there are neighborhood cats. In neighborhoods, residents feed them leftovers, usually dry bread soaked with stew. Some people provide shelter in their homes. One can see containers of food along streets placed where cats usually visit. Milk is intended for kittens.

Our family had a cat—this was over fifty years ago at this point! He was home most of the time. But when he was not, we knew he was safe at one of the neighbors' homes. We played with him, fed him, but most of all he wanted to lay around and be outside. He needed the opportunity to climb walls and run around, which he was not allowed to do in the house.

We moved from Morocco to the United States in 1989 and settled with our kids in Pennsylvania. We are now retired in Palm Desert. We love it here! In Pennsylvania, we were mostly working, and now we have time to enjoy ourselves playing tennis, swimming, and other activities. The weather, of course, is different. I felt at home quickly because Palm Desert reminds me of Marrakech, my birthplace—the weather, the mountains, the palm trees, all the vegetation, and now during spring, the scent of citrus blossoms.

When we were asked to watch Aaron and Lacy, we accepted right away, then thought *what have we done!?* We didn't know anything about living with cats in the United States. At first we felt it would be a big responsibility—what if they leave the house and get

lost? What if they get sick? It has been about one year now and they are a big part of our lives.

Both Lacy and Aaron have let us get to know them and their wants, likes, and dislikes. My husband and I have been acting like we have young kids again, taking pictures of their actions and calling each other when they do something new. They are comfortable with both of us, but Lacy is more attached to Christian and Aaron to me. In the morning, Lacy walks over to Christian, sits on top of his laptop keyboard, and looks up and waits for a conversation and petting. Aaron likes when I scratch his back, runs around a few times, and comes to lay close to me, sometimes so close so I can't move my arm to use the laptop keyboard, as though asking for my attention.

We had two dogs in the past, and having cats is very different. They definitely have changed our opinion about living with cats, especially because we never thought we'd ever have one at home after retiring. We like how independent cats are. And for me, it is so heartwarming seeing how Aaron and Lacy interact. It is surprising to me how communicative, smart, and affectionate they are, and how loving and caring they are for each other.

Amina Kim grew up in Marrakech, Morocco. She served as senior director of development for a leading real estate and community development company in central Pennsylvania for twenty-five years before retiring to Palm Desert, California.

Julie Newmar

Julie Newmar became famous for her portrayal of Catwoman on the 1960s TV series *Batman*, and the skintight costume that went along with it. The catsuit was made from a shiny, stretchy material called Lurex, which Newmar customized herself, slinging a gold belt around her hips instead of the waist. Though she was only on the show for six episodes, she gave young girls in the 1960s someone to look up to, as there weren't many strong, empowered women on television at the time, and she opened the door for many female actors to play the now iconic role.

On Prehistoric Cats

AN INTERVIEW WITH JUDY SMITH

As Adil and I visited local businesses in our new town, one thing I noticed everywhere were old photos of the properties. Every place had several framed snapshots from the 1950s and '60s when Borrego Springs had become a desert resort town hot spot and hideaway for Hollywood stars. Our neighbor, the Palms Hotel, had practically an exhibition installed in its lobby. Images of every movie star who had stayed there on one wall; I recognized only Marilyn Monroe. A glass display case held many more prints of glamorous men and women lounging poolside amid the mid-century decor.

I loved seeing these photos, and we soon discovered our own trove, hidden in a stuffed filing cabinet. There were men in '70s-era tracksuits standing in front of our property before the ground was paved, and a group of women smiling courtside while holding some of the first metal rackets. We didn't know their names, or where they were now, but they were here, and now we were, too. It made everything feel a little less insignificant; we were carrying on a legacy simply by being in Borrego Springs, and one day our photos would also be a part of history.

Most people in Borrego Springs were incredibly welcoming and eager to show off the town they loved so much. We met a woman named Judy Smith who worked at the state park's paleontology lab and offered to give us a tour. When we first entered the lab, we were greeted by a mass of dirt, plaster, and foil. Nestled in there was the skull of a mammoth that had recently been excavated.

Seeing these fossils and learning about the distant past immediately erased the high I'd been on from the old photos. So many animals had walked this land before I did, ones whose species did not even exist anymore. I examined the skull of a saber-toothed cat. What was it like being alive as this particular cat in the Anza-Borrego Desert millennia ago? Our lives would come and go just as quickly as his had. We were insignificant. Maybe I had to cling to feeling like a part of recent history so that the vastness of everything else didn't overwhelm and obliterate me. Rationally, I knew I was a speck, but if I was going to be happy on a day-to-day basis I had to forget that fact.

On display near the saber-toothed cat skull was a skeleton of a modern-day mountain lion, and next to that, a replica of a skeleton of an ordinary domestic cat. Smith had known the mountain lion, or at least her story. The lion had a tracker implanted so they were able to study her life; before she died, she was known for killing more sheep in the area than any other mountain lion. I wanted to know more, and Smith filled me in on the lives and legacies of the park's cats.

Smith: I've volunteered at Anza-Borrego's Paleo Lab for eighteen years now. I've really enjoyed that you can have different phases of what you work on until you find out what you really like. I started out doing mostly field, then I did mostly cleaning, and now I'm working more on organizing the collections. There are all kinds of different cats found here in the park. We have many cat bones in the collection, and we're able to measure the length of the bones to give us the size of the cats. Their size depends on their environment and how they hunt, whether they live in a forest, a savanna, or half and half. Small cats include the bobcat, ocelot, and river cat. They lived here 4.8 million to 700,000 years ago. A medium-sized cat, the American Cheetah, inhabited North America for about two million years and at about 156 pounds he was smaller than other known cheetahs.

Different species of cats hunt their prey in different ways, and again this is often determined by the landscape. Pursuit cats chase their prey, and ambush cats hide and then pounce. Today the Anza-Borrego region is a desert, but millions of years ago the

landscape shifted from forested to grasslands. Small cats that were here were adapted to living in woodsy areas with all the vegetation offering cover. As we move into the two- to three-million year range, the Borrego Valley starts drying out, becoming very similar to an African savanna, with open grasslands, rivers, and lakes. Cats who lived in the grasslands were mostly pursuit hunters—there weren't a lot of places to hide.

Today, the mountain lions live up in the rocky areas and hunt the sheep up there. The landscape is more barren than in the past, but there are still trees and bush and grass for them to hide in. You can observe how long the tail is on the modern-day mountain lion, as well as the house cat. If you go to the zoo or to the wild in Africa you'll see that the lions and cheetahs all have large tails. The tail is used as a way to keep balance when they're running and making quick turns. The mountain lions in the park chase bighorn sheep so their tails are long and the attachments for the muscles are a lot smaller. They're made for running.

The bobcat, on the other hand, has a short tail. He is one that hides and then pounces on its prey. Cats are very adaptable to where the food is. The bobcats here love the mobile home community, called the Roadrunner. A lot of people with pets in there put out cat food or dog food. If you don't have to kill anything and you can sit on a fence and watch them put out food and jump down and go get it— how easy is that!

Like a bobcat, the tail of the saber-toothed cat is short. There is a big debate whether they were scavengers or killed their own meat. Their saber teeth were very thin; if they bit into something and hit bone they probably broke easily. But you have to realize there was a lot of muscle attachment around the teeth so they were likely a lot stronger than they look. You can even see how large the house cat's incisors are compared to its other teeth. Several experiments have been run on how the saber-toothed cat could have killed its prey but none of them were conclusive, so we really don't know.

We do know what they looked like. With their heavy bones, stocky muscle attachments, and short tail it's a safe bet to say they pounced on their prey. Like today's mountain lion, the saber-tooth hunted prey bigger than itself. The mountain lion hunts the bighorn sheep, and the saber-tooth even went after mammoths.

Most people use the name "saber-toothed tiger" but the truth is we don't know if he was a tiger or not because no skin or hair remains. We don't know what its fur looked like and we don't know the markings on the fur. In some renderings it looks more like a leopard, but it's all imagined. Leopards, tigers, and cheetahs all have different spots or stripes. Lions don't have any—the male has a black mane, but basically they match the vegetation so that they can hide. "Tiger" probably became popularized in the 1800s when they started really studying bones, but at that time knowledge was only beginning. A lot of the English were discovering bones in India where tigers were plentiful. You only had people's imaginations on what to call this thing. It's big, it looks like a tiger. People are always going off of what they know and trying to make it fit. That's my guess, but I have no idea! Nowadays we call it the saber-toothed cat, and maybe at some time in the future something will be found with some skin on it that will further our knowledge. There is some skin from mammoths and mastodons that were trapped in the ice up in Siberia, so it is possible.

Judy Smith lives in Borrego Springs, California, where she has volunteered at the Anza-Borrego Paleontology Lab for the past eighteen years.

Siam the Siamese

The Siamese are one of the oldest breeds of Asians cats, originating in Siam, present-day Thailand. They were considered royalty, even sacred, as they roamed freely around Buddhist temples and perched atop palace walls. As early as the sixteenth century, Siamese cats were exported to the rest of the world.

In 1878, the first Siamese cat to ever reach America was sent to First Lady Lucy Hayes by David B. Sickels, a U.S. diplomat visiting the consulate in Bangkok. "I have taken the liberty of forwarding you one of the finest specimens of Siamese cats that I have been able to procure in this country," he wrote to her in a letter. Named Siam for her birthplace, the cat quickly made herself at home in the White House, wandering the halls as she pleased, entertaining the staff, and becoming close companions with twelve-year-old First Daughter Fanny Hayes.

Tragically, her tenure in the White House did not last long. Siam became gravely ill in the fall of 1879. The staff tried feeding her every kind of meat, fish, poultry, and milk they had to no avail, and then sent for the president's personal physician. She passed away just days later, leaving the entire staff and First Family in mourning.

Needing Physical Affection

GRACE LEE

My drive for physical affection had led me to a place where I thought I'd never go: a phone call from my gyno about a positive diagnosis. That effectively ended a career where I would slut around *without insisting* on condom usage; by age twenty, I'd enter a new phase where I'd slut around *insisting* on condom usage. Physical affection was a daft pursuit, I needed the temporary comforts of a hookup to feel a confectionary kind of love.

Slutting around was easy. With friends, I was an open book, talking smells and sizes. With these boys, I kept my mouth shut. The potential rejection was something I had no emotional capacity for. The little I had was reserved for the cat, Blondie, who was waiting for me at home.

I was at a bar with my friends, Proudlock and John. Before, over tacos, we were complaining to each other about our loneliness.

"I haven't had a boyfriend in five years," I'd complain after gulps of spicy margarita.

"Well, I haven't had a girlfriend," John said. His Welshness made girlfriend sound like there was no vowel between the g and the r.

Proudlock was more tight-lipped about his girl troubles, but he admitted that he had had only five partners.

Both musicians, they had their own legion of fans. They were both over six-feet tall and at 5'1", I had to jog to keep up with their pace on to the next bar. I didn't harbor anything bawdy toward them, although I wouldn't kick Proudlock out of bed. I felt secure when he hugged me and how his resting face read thoughtful.

John saw someone he knew and walked away, and Proudlock and I were sitting side by side on a ledge, drinking beers.

Proudlock wailed, "I wanna cuddle," and rubbed his one thousand kg head on my shoulder. Nodding my head, I thought, *Why would he say that to me? I would die to cuddle. I'm so lonely.* Proudlock was in New York City for a year to write songs. John introduced us and we were fast friends, texting about new bands and drinking at shows together.

He asked me where I lived and if I liked it there. I continued to sip my beer and eventually took a cab home.

The depression was all-consuming. I had a car salesman's affectation at school and work, but I was struggling to survive every day; I was obsessed with how to end my life. The selfishness protected me from boys and the inevitable pain they caused, and also prevented any kind of real connection with them. Inadvertently treating them as objects, the blanket-sized space between us would grow even wider.

I tainted a hook-up situation in Baltimore, where I was sleeping with the Internet crush of my dreams, a LiveJournal boy who called himself Baltimore Charlie. I was enamored looking at the self-portrait Polaroids he'd take in places I'd never been to around the United States. He was wayward and left his parents' house at seventeen, opposite of my suburban life. Baby-faced and going to a New York college, I met him at a party and we bonded over being Marylanders and missing home. We hooked up one summer after his friend's party in a Bolton Hill row house and I didn't see him for months.

We started to hang out again over the holidays, because we'd always have disappointing Christmases with our respective families. He lived in the Copycat (real name), a cavernous, swampy warehouse building in Baltimore that was home to musicians and artists. I liked his gruff voice and how he'd cross his legs when he smoked.

We'd talk about our own depressions and our despair regarding our fathers, but never the feelings we might have for each other. I would ramble about the cat I had adopted and the cute way she'd fall asleep, belly up.

When I got the positive diagnosis, I called him.

"Hey. My doctor called me. I think it's from you."

"Grace, I'm so sorry. I'll get tested right away."

The idea that he might care for me made me ache with a pain I didn't recognize.

My calico cat, Blondie, was the only companion who wouldn't judge. A short-haired white, gray, and orange tabby, she had a little pooch of a belly that suggested previous motherhood. She used to live on a soap opera extra's deck and he recognized that she was too special to be a street cat. She was so needy for attention and affection and that suited me, because I needed to be needed. Cat suffocation is disliked by cat haters, but that was the way to win over my cat-ambivalent heart. She'd lay on me for full days, when I'd leave bed only to pee.

Blondie was the only cat I ever loved. Most cats, I don't like. When they hide. The hissing. The plain meanness that some of them possess—nope. I don't like that some of them are gorgeous and fluffy, but they bear a personality so rotten they might as well be demons. Not interested.

Blondie, she was saccharine. So serene. Yes, on occasion, she liked to play and do that weird, possessed-ghost walk, but she loved to love me the most. If I sat on the toilet, she jumped on my lap. If I didn't come home at night, she'd wait for me by the front door the next day and follow me to my room. Anytime I'd lie down, she'd be right on my chest or in the crook of my neck. She was my tricolored shadow.

I was nineteen when I adopted her. In contrast to the sleepovers with boys, she sustained me every day with her eight pounds of unconditional love. The cat turned out to be my lifeline.

I'm thirty-one now. My dog, Penelope, is napping on the bed I share with my boyfriend of four years. After two firings, one layoff, a hundred failed interviews, and a thousand Tinder dates, I've survived rejection. My depression has been assuaged by antidepressants, therapy, and specialized therapy. Ultimately, the heartbreak over putting down Blondie put me in more pain than any boy. Her vet bills had amounted to a cost I couldn't afford as a college student and it was the only thing I could do, rather than let her suffer.

Depression is a beast but it was no match against a chubby calico. Blondie made me grateful to be alive to take care of her. She did redeem cats for me, too. But only the attention-starved ones.

Grace Lee lives in Brooklyn, New York. She studied at the New School and now works in brand marketing.

My First Big Loss

SAMHITA MUKHOPADHYAY

I know I'm lucky that my first big brush with losing a loved one was with an extremely cute furry friend, my black cat Guillermo. My best friend Rebekah and I had adopted him with his sister Guapa on a whim in Berkeley. We had just moved to the Bay Area with another friend and Rebekah's boyfriend. It was also a few months after September 11 and we were four New Yorkers craving home.

None of us really realized the commitment a set of cats required. We were young and irresponsible. When we split up as roommates it became clear that no one wanted to take the cats. So I took them and moved into an old house in Oakland that I'm sure was haunted. The two cats protected me in that house of evil spirits (filled with great and extremely generous people).

It was a transient time in my life but having two cats kept me grounded. I moved about four times while I had these cats and lost one of them in the process. We three first moved to the outer Mission neighborhood of San Francisco. Then we moved to Haight-Ashbury. This is where I lost Guapa. I cried and waited for her for days and days and searched every log of every shelter for weeks but no sign of her. We never knew what happened to Guapa—did she run away? Was she kidnapped? We'll never know.

Then it was just the two of us, me and Guillermo. Guillermo and I moved in with my boyfriend who loved him as much as I did. It was why I loved my boyfriend so much, too. And when the relationship ended, Guillermo and I moved out on our own. I was heartbroken, but I had Guillermo. Guillermo moved with me again and then again to New York to live with my parents while I put my life back together and worked on my first book.

Guillermo was my first, chosen, and most consistent love. He was my rock.

A few days after my thirty-first birthday, Guillermo stopped walking. We took him to get X-rays but it wasn't really clear why he couldn't walk. We had the option to give him an MRI but some cats go into seizures from MRIs. Also, it cost three thousand dollars and I didn't even have health insurance for myself.

We hoped and prayed for Guillermo to get better. Soon he stopped being able to urinate on his own. The vet was able to manually express him. I taught myself how to as well. My mom helped (also a cat lady, mother of all cat ladies to be honest). When I was traveling for work she would run him to the vet every day to get him expressed.

I never considered myself a cat lady, but I would have done anything to keep Guillermo alive.

The thing with animals is they can't communicate their pain. I didn't know if he was in pain and I didn't know if I could trust myself to let him go for his sake. So I would ask the vet over and over (and there were many trips to the vet) if I was hanging on too long. She reassured me I was not, and if he were in pain he wouldn't still purr and cuddle and love us so much. He'd stop eating.

I searched the Internet and talked to friends for answers. How do you know when to let go? Those who were skeptics said I should have already while others told me I would know, to trust myself, and that I would make the right choice.

As this was happening, I was planning my ninth move with Guillermo to an apartment in Brooklyn. We had successfully landed in New York and were ready to venture out of the comforts of my parents' home.

The night before my move he had stopped eating. He didn't want to make eye contact anymore. I got the message. He didn't want to make another move, he had had it, it was his time to go. He knew it, I knew it, we all knew it. I have never had to make such a difficult

decision, but somehow had the strength and clarity of mind to make it.

Guillermo had taught me that. He taught me to love and when to let go of that love. And as I held him in his last dying moments as they put him to sleep, I felt a pang of loss I had never felt before. That deep realization that you can intellectualize the pain of loss but don't truly know it until it happens to you. That the things and people we love are temporary, that they can go at any time.

It's been ten years since Guillermo died. It took me that long to get a new cat (I just did!). But I'm also facing a sick father at the end of his life. It's not the same and I'm not going to pretend it is. But losing Guillermo taught me to understand the magnitude and tectonic shift in your life that is the loss of a loved one. That it's important to take your time with it, to let yourself wallow in the unfairness of it, and to accept that loss is inevitable.

And despite that loss, you will be OK on the other side. For such a tiny creature, it still confounds me that Guillermo was able to do all that.

Samhita Mukhopadhyay is a New York City–based writer, editor, speaker, and digital strategist. She is currently _Teen Vogue_'s executive editor.

Acknowledgments

This book was truly a group effort. Many thanks to everyone who worked on it: my agent Kate Woodrow, editor Holly La Due, designer Adil Dara, Anjali Pala and Ayesha Wadhawan at Prestel, and every writer and interviewee who contributed a piece. I also must thank my cats Aaron and Lacy for sitting with me for hours while I painted, scanned, wrote, and edited!

© Prestel Verlag, Munich · London · New York 2019
A member of Verlagsgruppe Random House GmbH
Neumarkter Strasse 28 · 81673 Munich

Prestel Publishing Ltd.
14-17 Wells Street
London W1T 3PD

Prestel Publishing
900 Broadway, Suite 603
New York, NY 10003

Library of Congress Cataloging-in-Publication Data

Names: Goren, Leah, author.
Title: Catlady : a love letter to women and their cats / Leah Goren.
Description: Munich ; New York : Prestel Publishing, [2020]
Identifiers: LCCN 2019033299 | ISBN 9783791385990 (hardcover)
Subjects: LCSH: Cat owners--Anecdotes. | Cats--Anecdotes.
Classification: LCC SF442.7 .G67 2020 | DDC 636.8--dc23
LC record available at https://lccn.loc.gov/2019033299

A CIP catalogue record for this book is available from the British Library.

Editorial direction: Holly La Due
Design and layout: Adil Dara
Production: Anjali Pala
Copyediting: John Son
Proofreading: Kelli Rae Patton

Verlagsgruppe Random House FSC® N001967
Printed on the FSC®-certified paper

Printed in China
ISBN 978-3-7913-8599-0
www.prestel.com